A Life of School
by
Colin Millar

Published by Colin Millar 2003

Acknowledgements

The cutting, "Charlie's Doggone Lucky" and the picture of The First XV v The Masters in 1951 are published with permission of The Bristol Evening Post.

The Picture of "Cliffside was a collection of wooden buildings" is published courtesy of Richard Goodall the son of the artist.

The photograph of our wedding is published courtesy of Chris Bromhead.

I have been unable to trace the photographer who took photographs of my mother, my father and of me displaying an enquiring mind.

Should I inadvertently have published any other copyright material I can only apologise and make corrections in any future printings.

ISBN 0 9546179 0 8

Printed by Zenith Media

A LIFE OF SCHOOL

Index

A LIFE OF SCHOOL 1933 TO 2000

You might call these the ramblings of a Mr Chips. Certainly they are the reminiscences of a Schoolmaster, and I use the old-fashioned term rather than 'Teacher' because I myself am old-fashioned. My story doesn't pretend to be special, but it covers a period when enormous changes took place – changes that surely could never have been envisaged seventy or more years ago when I first appeared on the scene. My hope is that parts of this book will entertain, and also touch a chord here and there with those who might read what I have to say. This is not intended to be the story of my life. These are my memories. Some may have become more coloured with the passing of time, others may have become more dimmed. Chronologically the order may not always be correct, but I have been as faithful to fact as my memory will allow. I have tried to avoid mentioning anything that might offend. Should I have failed I can only ask forgiveness. I have sought help of various friends to verify much of what I have written. I would particularly like to thank the following: Gill ('Sweetie' my wife) without whose help and encouragement this book would not have seen the light of day; David and Tricia Exell, who kindly read through and corrected an early script; Julia Morris, Gill's niece, for her help and for introducing me to Peter Marks of Zenith Media, who in turn has helped me through the intricacies of the printer's world. I would also like to thank Catherine Mercer, John Sanson of Redcliffe Press and Trevor Hockey of Clifton Bookshop, for help as I mulled over whether to publish or not. Thanks are due too to Nigel Sommerville for guidance over legal aspects of the book, Jim Lodge for confirming some of the details of my time in Canada, Tom Gover of the Old Cliftonian Society, Dr Bob Acheson the Headmaster of Clifton College Preparatory School, Richard Tovey the Headmaster of Tockington Manor School, Ian Barlow and John Bradbury. I have also received help from my sister Annie Cole, who dug out the old family albums from the attic, Bar Rushton who furnished me with information about my mother before she was married and also Mary Hall and Christine Martin and others who unearthed for me, not only the name of the lip-reading teacher I had when I was at University, but also gave me much interesting information about her of which I was unaware - to all of those mentioned I am greatly indebted. If I have left anyone out - please forgive me. I hasten to add though that in no way can any of the people mentioned above be blamed for anything that I have written.

Although I have never been wealthy in financial terms this has been made up for in the quality of life that I have enjoyed. There have been sad moments and difficult times, but they have been more than made up by happy memories and I hope this will be evident in the following pages.

1st November 2003

Chapter 1 - Early Days

I know little about my early days except that I was the first child of Joy and Dusty Millar. I was born on 16th October 1933. My place of birth was Uxbridge because that is where my father, an accountant with the Air Ministry, worked. I still know little about Uxbridge - possibly there isn't much to know, though no doubt the good citizens of Uxbridge would put me right on that! At any rate the first five years of my life didn't, on reflection, seem to make any great impression on my life except in two ways. Firstly,

Papa. (after he was wounded)

I acquired a sister, Ann, two and a bit years after I had arrived in the world.

Secondly during the first year or two of my life I picked up an ear infection which resulted in me being hard of hearing. This is something I have had to live with for the rest of my life, and I suppose that if there was one thing that I would have changed in my life it would have been to have had perfect hearing. But more about that later.

My parents were wise, kind, gentle, loving and totally unselfish. We were in a sense cocooned and yet in a way we had much more freedom than children today.

My father was 87 years old when he died in 1979. He was a man of great integrity who was loved and respected by all who came in touch with him.

Like so many of his generation, his life was very much affected by the Great War. When war broke out in 1914 he was just 22 years old. He served as an Officer in the Civil Service Rifles and eventually ended up as a Captain. He was modest about his achievements and never spoke of the horrors that he had inevitably faced. He survived just - although he was badly wounded, suffered septicemia which was, of course, far more serious in those pre-penicillin days than now. After some two years in hospital he was invalided out, but with his right arm fixed at a right angle and two of his fingers set straight. As a child the arm was a source of considerable interest and my sister and I quickly realised its potential as a hook for carrying surplus coats if we got too hot on our walks at weekends. I have always been under the impression that he had been due to transfer to the Army Air Corps the day after he was wounded.

My mother was several years younger than my Father. She too was much loved by all who came in contact with her. I know little about her early life, but that her mother died when she was relatively young and she didn't get on with her step mother or her step sisters. That is not to say that she had an unhappy childhood. Her father was in Cable and Wireless and so her parents spent much time in foreign parts. She had a spell in Gibraltar which she loved, and was at school at a convent there for a

My mother was much loved

while. Later she was sent to a boarding school in Bushey, Hertfordshire, where she made friends with whom she kept in touch for the rest of her life. One was later to become my god-mother at whose wedding I was page boy. She always spoke of the school and the headmistress there with affection. Because travel in those days was by comparison with today so pedestrian, virtually the only time she met up with her parents was in the summer. These summer holidays, spent in Gib, Madeira and other places after a leisurely cruise were generally happy times. Holidays, except when she went to see her parents were spent with a favourite aunt in Ealing. After she left school she apparently struck up a liaison with a young man who was deemed to be unsuitable. As her father was working in Aden at the time it was arranged that some friends, who had also been posted to Aden, should take her with them. It was there that she met my father, and, eventually, a year or two later married him.

Within a year or two of being born we moved to the lovely area that was to become the family home for almost the rest of our lives - namely the Goring Gap, the area where the Berkshire Downs almost meet the Chilterns, but are just separated by a silver thread that is the Thames.

The first home that I remember, and that only vaguely, was Sunfield, which was situated at the bottom of Townsend Road in Streatley. This was just over the river from Goring. I don't recall a great deal about the house, but it did have a gate which I am reliably informed I was able to climb over at an early age. Fortunately I was always caught before I had gone very far. It was this natural ability and instinct for climbing that got me into trouble a few years later, but of that more anon. In those days we didn't have a car, so inevitably we walked everywhere, even down to the shops in Goring. As a toddler, of course, I was forever falling down and it was customary to have the damage kissed better. This could prove quite embarrassing. When I sat down rather heavily on one of our shopping expeditions, I bared the damaged area and refused to budge until I had had the tender area kissed better.

In those early days of our life as a family we led a rather restless existence. In 1938 we moved to Reading for what ever reason I know not. I went to a small kindergarten school there where I was introduced to the joys of DIY.

I made a wooden house - as I remember, it was a block of wood with a few nails banged in to it, which I painted bright red, but such was my lack of artistic finesse that I suspect that I was covered with as much paint as the model was.

A few months later, Father was posted out to Aden again. So the family plus Nanny, Evelyn, set off on the Rasputana through the Straits of Gibraltar across the Mediterranean Sea and finally through the Suez Canal. The journey was a happy interlude and passed without incident, except that I did give my parents a run for their money at Port Said. There various traders and entertainers came on board among them a Gullie Gullie man. I had observed a crowd on one of the decks and when I had a chance managed to give my parents the slip. Being only four or five years old and small I found it wasn't difficult to smuggle myself to the front of the crowd who were watching this magician produce chicks out of thin air. Eventually my parents, who were getting fairly frantic, spotted me and I was severely reprimanded!

Mine was an enquiring mind

I have many happy memories of our time in Aden, and some less agreeable. We seemed to live in various homes during our year there. At one stage we stayed in a hotel. For me one of the advantages of this was that a Royal Marines Band performed their marching routine just in front of the hotel - what could be more exciting for a five-year-old boy! There was a

4

considerable ex-pat community in Aden at the time so there was quite a lot going on. Occasionally the normal routine was interrupted by a visit of a Royal Navy ship. I suspect this was often an excuse for a party. The children were catered for as well as the adults. I remember on one occasion an invitation was extended to guests to go down in a diving suit. One lady tried this. I don't know what she saw when she reached the bottom, or whether she simply got over-excited. At all events she fainted and had to be hauled up in an inert state and revived.

Much time was spent at a beach that was wired off to protect swimmers from marauding sharks. I could only swim under the water. This was fine till I ran out of air, when I would surface gasping for breath. I was rarely out of my depth. On one occasion though, a group of us were fishing from a pontoon way out in the bay and I fell in. I spluttered to the surface. Fortunately outstretched hands were there to pull me back on board.

I suspect our favourite house that year was 'The Bungalow'. While living there my sister and I were the proud owners of a small goat. We must have lived in some style at the time because we had an ayah who couldn't do anything right as far as I was concerned, and various other servants. My refusal to do what the ayah, probably quite reasonably, requested was one of the rare occasions when my parents were angry with me and I was sentenced to solitary confinement in my room for a short while.

Opposite 'The Bungalow', there was, as I recall, a lovely beach. But it was always impressed upon us that we should be very careful going into the sea here. It was certainly off-limits to swimmers. But even paddling was something that we only did with care because of the danger of attack from sharks. They sometimes swam in fairly shallow water and were quite capable of grabbing an unsuspecting paddling toddler. The occasional limbless Arab that one saw was a salutary reminder of the damage that sharks inflicted.

Aden was hot, very hot. I was not allowed out of doors without my Topee. This much-hated piece of headgear was the first thing I disposed of when it was no longer needed. As soon as we cleared the Suez Canal on our journey home it was ceremoniously consigned to the sea! Whether I did in fact go

Ann and me wearing the hated topees
outside Government House

outside without it on one occasion, or whether I became dehydrated, or suffered from the heat for some other reason is not clear. But I know that I ended up in a hospital with what was diagnosed as Heatstroke. I spent three weeks in the hospital, and it was probably three weeks too long as far as I was concerned. But I did enjoy the staple diet of jelly and wafer biscuits.

I think I must have been a timid youngster, because, aged about five, I was taken to see my first moving picture. We sat fairly close to the screen. Whether it featured Donald Duck or some other duck, I am not sure. But from the front row the ducks on screen were gigantic and when they actually quacked the amplified sound combined with their huge size was too much for me. I was not happy and demanded to be taken home.

Another of those rare occasions when I incurred the wrath of my parents was when we moved to Government House briefly. This was great fun. I soon observed that every time we as a family went in or out of the main gates the guards presented arms. So when I could escape the watchful eyes of those who were looking after me, I went off to the main entrance to see if the guard would present arms to me. They did. But my joy was all too

6

brief. My parents soon caught up with me and were not amused. I was probably given another term of solitary confinement! Anyway I did not attempt to do it again.

Later on during our stay in Aden war was looking increasingly likely and it was decided that practice should be carried out with the anti-aircraft guns. Unfortunately the guns were sited just outside the house. The noise was considerable and I was extremely nervous, so much so, that when subsequent practices were scheduled I was hastily moved to somewhere on the other side of town

In fact just before my sixth birthday the threat of war and the vulnerability of Aden became such that we were evacuated to Mombassa, not before we had had a party to celebrate my forthcoming birthday because, "None of my friends would be in Mombassa". However we weren't in Mombassa for many days before the powers that be decided we were no safer there than back in Aden. So we returned to Aden in time to celebrate my birthday on the actual day! Soon after that it was deemed unsafe to stay in Aden too, so we packed up and sailed home. We left in late December. The ship, I remember had a searchlight and a small gun - as protection against enemy activity I suppose, but I suspect it would have been of little use if we had been confronted by an enemy action of any kind. The journey to Marseilles passed without incident.

I can still picture us standing around in a disconsolate way on the railway tracks at Marseilles. Although the adults did not voice their fears to the children, they appeared distracted and very worried. This part of France had not fallen, but no doubt there was some concern as to whether we would make it to one of the channel Ports and so to Southampton. We did make it, but arriving in January 1940 - one of the coldest winters on record - having come from the heat of Aden, with no home to go to was not a happy experience. We holed up in a hotel in Southampton for a short while, before some friends kindly offered us somewhere to lay our heads in a house in Stonehouse, Gloucestershire.

We spent a year in Stonehouse. I'm not sure how successful this was. The other family was made up of parents and three girls. In fact my father and the girls' father were not there very much. My father spent the week in London and the girl's father probably did the same. At any rate I was surrounded by women, which I wasn't too sure about. There were the occasional exciting interludes when "Uncle Bernard", who was a dispatch-rider in the army, used to appear on his motor cycle.

The all-female environment was also relieved by the fact that I was sent off to a local boys' Preparatory School. Here I learned to read and write. I had had little formal teaching before that. I owe quite a considerable debt of gratitude to a Miss Wright who gave me my educational grounding, particularly in the basics of the three Rs.

Every morning I walked to school. It wasn't very far, but it involved walking past the school chapel which had been severely damaged in a fire. I was very frightened that the remaining structure would collapse so I always ran past it as quickly as I could, to reduce the chance of it falling on me.

I do remember if we were naughty we had to run round one of the playing fields - how many times depended on how naughty we were. We had a little bit of a walk to the building where we had our lunch. There, before we could start to eat our lunch, we had to wash, do our hair and then we were subjected to rigorous scrutiny. By the time I had smarmed my hair down and combed it, I apparently looked too much like Adolf Hitler, so my comb was confiscated. I suspect this did not worry me unduly.

The school had an outdoor pool where, despite the fact that the temperature was considerably colder than the sea temperature in Aden, I learned to swim on the surface instead of below it.

Our sojourn in Gloucestershire only lasted a brief year and then we moved back to the area we had lived in before going to Aden.

Chapter 2 – By the River

Our new home was in a rambling house by the Thames, about a quarter of a mile above Goring Lock. It was an idyllic spot for a small boy. I was barely eight years old when we moved in. The flat wasn't self contained and was not very smart, but it was our home and we didn't have to share it with anyone else. The house belonged to a renowned Botanist and collector of plants, by name of Kingdom Ward, but we never saw him. This was either because he was always away collecting plants, fighting for his country or engaged in some other activity.

The attraction of this new home for me was the large slightly run down garden and its proximity to the river. In fact a small lake in the grounds emptied into the river. Astride the narrow channel that connected the lake to the river was a boathouse and it was from the little walkway at one end of the boathouse that linked the two sides of the channel that I spent many happy hours staring down into the murky waters trying to catch the perch that swam there. I would dangle my line with a tempting worm on the end. I did catch fish occasionally and even ate one of two of my prizes, but generally I was not a very successful fisherman.

I had the run of this huge garden. There was even a walled kitchen garden, where I remember experiencing both excitement and terror when I spotted an adder in a row of lupins.

The garden contained a Mulberry tree, so keeping silkworms was a brief hobby, but we never did accumulate enough silk to make anything. Being war time meant that everything was very scarce and of course rationing was in operation. Nowadays, when we slap the butter on our toast with a gay abandon, unless we are concerned about cholesterol levels, it is hard to comprehend that in the war the weekly ration was just two ounces. Sometimes we supplemented that by making our own. It was quite simple. We took the cream off the top of the milk, put it in a jam jar and, having secured the top, shook it vigorously for what was probably only twenty minutes, but at the age of eight or nine, seemed like a lifetime. The butter eventually emerged. It was washed, salt was added and our weekly butter ration was considerably increased. It tasted extra special too because we had made it!

Ann on Stepping Stones at Cleeve Court

One winter the river over-flowed its banks and the house where we lived was almost severed from the outside world. A line of stepping stones was placed so that we could reach the outside world without getting our feet wet. When the flooding was followed by a period of sharp frost the fields downstream from us would freeze over and the area would become a popular skating venue. Because it was only a few inches deep it was completely safe too.

Although the house and its position had much to commend it there were some minuses as well. One we discovered fairly early on during our sojourn there and that was that we appeared to share it with a fairly large rat population. The cat, Sally, used to bring specimens into the living room at breakfast time. They seemed almost as large as she was, and although she was pleased with her efforts, the rest of us weren't so happy. On one occasion when mother went to bed she heard and felt a rat in the springs of her bed. After a while a 'Rat man' came and put down poison and as far as I can remember the rat population decreased dramatically.

I went to school at Moulsford, a few miles upstream. It was one of those schools that are intended for girls, but cater for a few small boys. My abiding memory of this school is being expelled! The building where we had our lessons was surrounded by grass, and there were dotted about a number of trees. Mine was an enquiring mind and I had developed a passion for climbing trees. Though I say it myself, I was rather good at it. On the fateful day, during a break from lessons, I was in the garden and I decided to climb what was, certainly from today's perspective, a fairly tall tree. It was probably a nest in it that captured my attention and that I needed to investigate. At any rate when one of the staff called to me to come down, I took no notice. Whether this was because I didn't hear or because I was too engrossed in the nest History does not relate. Whatever it was, the fact is that when my poor mother came to collect me later, she was devastated to be told that they could not keep me any longer. I would have to leave.

Not surprisingly my mother was very upset that her little boy had been expelled. Such an event had a much more serious stigma attached to it in those days. However as luck would have it there lived in the same building as us a delightful old lady -she seemed old to me – but she was probably only in her forties - who just happened to be the Headmistress of a similar school to the one from which I had been evicted, but it was five miles in the other direction. She tactfully told my mother she had always wanted me to go to her school!

So for the next two or three years I went to Pangbourne PNEU School. As I remember it, I was very happy there, and eventually I was prepared for Clifton, where I went as soon as the War ended. The journey to the school at Pangbourne involved a walk of two miles from our home, through the estate, past the Streatley cricket ground, past the Veterinary College farm and Streatley Church, over the bridge that crosses the Thames and joins Going to Streatley and up the High Street to the Station. Today it seems almost unbelievable that, aged 8, I should have regularly made this journey accompanied, after a year or two, only by my little sister. It was even more surprising that I never missed the train, although there were the odd occasions when the guard, who could hear me pounding over the footbridge, forebore to wave his green flag until I was safely on board. I and one or two others who joined me at Goring & Streatley Station were accompanied on the train by a strict lady who wouldn't allow me to look out of the window! I was very peeved about this and complained bitterly to my parents. Eventually I was allowed do the train part of the journey unsupervised! Even when we reached Pangbourne we still had another half a mile to walk.

The journey which I did every day whatever the weather was generally uneventful although I do remember one witch-like woman poking us with her umbrella as we waited on the station to come home - we had probably been noisy and irritating.

Occasionally on the return journey in the afternoon I would stop off at the Veterinary College farm to 'help' the Land girls with the milking of the cows. There were only a few animals, each was named, and had a stall of her own. When they were brought in from the field they always went straight to their own stall. Each knew exactly where to go. Then seated on traditional stools the girls would milk the cows by hand. Occasionally I was allowed to have a go.

I remember coming back from school one day to find a small detachment of American soldiers encamped close to the village cricket field. I can't recall how long they were there or how many there were of them. But they really did have chewing gum and Hershey's chocolate to give away!

Some time early on during our time in the house by the river I contracted Malta or Abortus Fever. Now known as Brucellosis, it is a low grade fever usually contracted as the result of eating contaminated dairy products in this case probably ice cream. Whatever the source of the illness I was quite poorly and it must have been a worrying time for my parents. I spent the best part of a whole term off school, which I did not enjoy, particularly as I wasn't well enough even to play out in the garden.

Because of the War we did various things to help the War effort or to help ourselves. My mother, who was a superb needle woman and knitter, joined up with a friend and ran a little dress-making business. This same friend also kept chickens so they (and we sometimes) had fresh eggs. Occasionally we would collect rosehips for jelly, or belladonna, which we were warned was very poisonous, and was used for medicines. At the top of Streatley Hill there was an area where brambles abounded and we had blackberrying expeditions. I didn't mind picking them, but I strongly objected to the climb up the steep hill. I wasn't too popular as a picker either as I consumed too many myself. The blackberries that did reach home were then boiled up and made into jam. We even collected little bits of sheep's wool that had clung on the barbed wire of fences.

When harvest time came round we assembled at Bishop's Farm to help. Most able-bodied men had gone off to war so all help was welcome. The fields had already been cut. This was quite an exciting business as there were usually quite a number of rabbits, hares and rats in the field. As the reaping machines went round and round the field, the uncut part became smaller and smaller. Eventually the small animals within this area had nowhere to hide and they would make a dash for freedom followed by a troop of men and boys hoping to bag something for the pot. There were field mice too. I don't remember trying to catch them, though I do remember picking one up. It took exception to being removed from its natural habitat and made its views known by sinking its teeth into my finger and holding on with a vice-like grip. I couldn't get rid of it fast enough. The reaping machines in those days cut the crop and bound it in sheaves. Our task was to pick the sheaves up and stand them in 'stooks', double rows of six or eight. Thus self supported the air could get at them and they would dry off, weather permitting. After a few days we would go round and rearrange the stooks so that the inside was on the outside. Eventually when deemed to be dry they would be loaded on to horse drawn wagons and taken off to the farmyard to be threshed.

One of the more popular jobs was that of leading the large cart horse that dragged the wagons. They were placid enough animals, but as I learned to my cost, it was important to make sure one's feet were not where the horse, which was huge and very heavy, was going to put his! While the horse was trundled round the field helpers with pitch forks would heave the sheaves on to the wagon. As I was only a little chap I was too small to heave the sheaves on to the wagon once a few layers had been stacked. I was, however, sometimes allowed on the wagon and I enjoyed the challenge of stacking the sheaves in an orderly fashion. There was a correct way of placing the sheaves, namely, evenly and with the heads of the crop facing inwards so that there was no danger of the load being shed on its way to the farm yard.

It was from Bishop's Farm that we had acquired our cat Sally. I had gone over to the farm on what was probably just a social visit. While there, I was shown some kittens and decided one would be a welcome addition to our family. I suspect mother did not greet her with open arms. But Sally became very much a part of the family and lived a long life. She eventually was run over by an electric float that used to deliver milk to us. She was then about twenty-two. At that age even milk floats moved too fast for her.

The river was always a source of pleasure. There was, of course, an abundance of wild life associated with it, and my love of the countryside stems from those days, and so too my fascination with running water. On warm summer days a favourite occupation was to go up to Cleeve Lock. The Lock keeper was a friendly man and he allowed us and one or two others to swim from his domain. In between dips I loved nothing better than to help open the large lock gates. First though the sluices had to be opened by turning wheels. The water would rush in or out depending on whether the boat was going upstream or downstream and when the level of water was the same on either side of the lock gate it would be heaved open. Once the boat was in the lock the procedure would be reversed and the other gates would be opened.

Later, when we moved to the other side of the river, we maintained our association with the Lock. To save us having to make the long journey round and over the bridge that connects the villages of Goring and Streatley, we would walk down to the bank opposite Cleeve Lock and shout loudly. The Keeper would hear cries and someone would row over to collect us.

Chapter 3 – Milverton and Other Homes

After two or three years by the river we were on the move again. We moved into a detached house over the bridge in Cleeve, which was really a part of Goring. The house, called Milverton, was not on the river itself. When we took possession in 1943 or 44, there was no electricity. The heating was in the form of open or gas fires. The lighting and the fridge too were run off gas. Gas in those days was made by the process of heating coal and was supplied by the local gasworks, which in this case, was just two or three hundred yards down the road. It was a smelly place and I think I must have been a little apprehensive that it might blow up at any moment, because I was always keen to pass it as quickly as possible. There was no electricity and, of course, no washing machines. As far as washing of clothes was concerned I suspect there was a fairly strict routine as in the song that we used to sing as children in school singing classes:

'Twas on a Monday morning

When I beheld my darling,

She looked so neat and charming

In ev'ry high degree.

She looked so neat and nimble, O,

A doing of her washing, O,

Dashing away with the smoothing iron,

She stole my heart away.

Tuesday was for hanging out the linen, Wednesday for starching, Thursday for ironing, Friday for folding, Saturday for airing and, of course, Sunday for wearing. Incidentally it was very frowned upon to hang clothes out on a Sunday.

Mother may not have had quite such a strict routine as that, but there was certainly a pattern. She used to boil the 'whites' in a big pot. A little blue dye was added to maintain their whiteness. Other clothes were washed in the bathroom, probably in the bath. If they were very dirty it was necessary to use the washboard, a corrugated board on which the clothes were scrubbed vigorously. Finally the clothes were passed through the mangle. As children we were urged to keep our fingers away from the rollers. But every now and then our curiosity and fascination got the better of us and we would put our fingers a little too close to the rollers with painful results.

As well as the gas works there was also a bakery and a cobbler's in the centre of the village. Both these places had very distinctive, but much more attractive, smells. It was a treat to go into the bakery especially if it was cold outside. As you opened the rather rickety wooden door you were greeted by the delicious smell of warm bread. However cold it was outside, the bakers would be perspiring as they toiled away kneading the dough and then putting it into the massive ovens with their long-handled tools. The cobbler worked in a wooden shed on the other side of the High Street. In the winter months heat was provided by a small coal or wood-burning stove in the middle of the building. The metal chimney from it went straight up through the roof. The stove didn't look very robust and with an array of combustible materials around it seemed something of a fire risk. I am sure today the Health and Safety Department would have had something to say. It was warm though. Fumes from the stove combined with the smell of leather to provide a cosy environment for the cobbler, who was a real craftsman, and for all who entered his workshop. Although he seemed to work in the middle of chaos, all around him were bits of leather and shoes, he must have had a system, because when one went to collect a pair of shoes that were being repaired they were always beautifully done and he always managed to locate them. There had been a brewery in the village too, though that had closed in 1939 and at that time I was not old enough to appreciate the merits of well-brewed beer.

During the early years that we lived in the area milk was delivered from the local dairy by horse-drawn float. Jugs and other small containers were put out by the customers and the milkman would ladle into these the correct amount of milk. The horse always seemed to know exactly where to stop and when to move on. I loved riding on the back of the milk-cart and helping the milkman deliver milk.

Although we were now living in Goring we still kept our association with Streatley in various ways. For example when I was a teenager I began to play cricket for Streatley. Home matches were played on the field not far from where we used to live. For away matches we would assemble at the Bull or some other appointed place and most of us would be transported in the lorry belonging to the local Road Haulier. My guess is that he was one of the few people who had fuel to run a vehicle. After the match there would be the ritual sinking of a few pints before we returned home in a fairly merry frame of mind. One fairly rotund gentleman used to down ten pints. As each pint disappeared the gentleman's face took on an ever deepening reddish colour. At the time I was fascinated how anyone could drink that much, though not surprised, when on the return journey, we had to make the occasional stop near suitable hedges.

To compensate for not being close to the river my parents in due course bought a small plot of river frontage about a mile away. It was something of a jungle - willows and bulrushes and other aquatic plants. It was approached by a steep bank, in which we hacked rustic steps, to enable us to reach the water's edge. We also had to make a small bridge to cross ha-ha that ran along the foot of the bank. This was a very basic construction being simply railway sleepers that were thrown across the small stream. 'The Plot' could hardly be called very smart, but was occasionally used for picnics and sometimes I would go down there for a spot of fishing. A small area by the river was seeded with grass so that we had somewhere to sit.

'The Plot' was also close to the local yacht club. I think we were members, but we didn't have a boat. Occasionally someone would

My parents bought a small plot of river frontage

need a crew and we would offer our services. There was one occasion, some years later when I was in my teens, when we had wandered down to the yacht club to find that there was a Juniors' Firefly competition on. The winner of the previous three years had passed on to senior ranks and competition was needed for the lad who had been runner up. Ann and I were pressed into taking part, so that the previous year's runner up could say that he had actually beaten someone. Unfortunately we spoilt the plot as we sailed home triumphant! It was the first time I had taken the helm of a boat, other than for brief spells when there was a clear river in front of us, and no tacking was involved. Needless to say the 'prospective' winner was not a happy lad and his father was furious.

Milverton itself was not very special, but it saw us through to the end of the war. As a child the war did not really touch my life, except that there wasn't an abundance of food, or anything else for that matter. Father would have seen more of it in London. In the country there were occasional air-raid warnings. The siren was situated on the local fire station. The noise it made was quite terrifying. On the occasions when I had to go past the fire station I moved very fast in case the siren started. Sometimes enemy planes would fly overhead probably to bomb Bristol or some other town west of us. There was one tragedy when a bomb fell on an isolated house by the river, and killed the occupants. It was pure chance and very bad luck as there wasn't another house anywhere near. One can only think that one of the German Bombers was getting rid of a bomb it hadn't dropped on the target.

We were always on the lookout for souvenirs of the war. If a German plane came down it was essential viewing, but souvenirs were scarce as the police or military would be quick to mount a guard. There was some excitement when strips of silver paper floated down from the sky. They were a collectable item for small boys. We understood that they were something to do with anti-radar, but quite what we never discovered.

There was excitement too when there was an army exercise involving dozens of planes towing gliders. From both planes and gliders floated down hundreds of parachutists to land in the fields behind our house. With hindsight I imagine this might have been some sort of rehearsal for the D-Day Landings.

Later, in the summer of 1944, numbers of our friends arrived at Milverton to escape from the "Doodlebugs", or V1 Rockets, to give them their correct name. These were an early form of guided missile launched by the Germans initially from Belgium and were terrifying. Apparently you could hear "Phut! Phut!" as they got closer and you could often see them. Then the engine would cut out and you knew you had 15seconds to get to a shelter. They not only wrought much damage but, certainly initially, also had an enormous psychological effect. I don't remember much about this influx of visitors except that Uncle Bill, who was not an uncle at all, but a good friend from Aden days, and his wife, didn't get on with some of the others. As far as I was concerned Uncle Bill could do little wrong. He had a workshop on the river at Hampton Court and produced for me a magnificent model sailing boat from drift wood he had fished out of the river. The boat was self steering and the theory was that it would always return to base. I never tested this theory too stringently, but the boat is still a treasured possession.

With warring factions at Milverton the family, and a cousin of my father's known to us as Auntie Bessie, decided to abandon them and go off on a boating holiday. By this time I was approaching twelve years old and Ann, my sister, ten. We hired a skiff with an awning like "The Three Men in a Boat" and a little dinghy, which I rowed, and set off upstream to Oxford. We also had a small tent. I can't recall much about the trip, except that we reached Oxford. While there we rowed up the Cherwell. On the way back to the main stream, I was in the lead in my dinghy when I spotted what looked very like a man's head just breaking the surface of the water. I went back to tell the family what I thought I had seen. This announcement was initially greeted with scepticism, but as they drew closer there was consternation and I was hurried on. Later my parents informed the police, and later still, by some years, I learned that what I had seen was the body of a student, who had tied weights of some sort to his feet and thrown himself into the river.

The return down river was uneventful. By the time we got home the doodlebug menace seemed to have abated a little. So the refugees, along with Auntie Bessie, dispersed and soon life returned to normal.

After the war ended we occasionally visited Auntie Bessie in her small detached house in Isleworth, opposite the school where she taught what was then called Domestic Science. She was a cousin of my father's, had grown up with him and was one of his few surviving relatives, although she had two or three brothers and a sister-in law who lived in Canada. During the war we occasionally received food parcels from them. I can't remember what they contained other than Chocolate bars - Hershey's I believe, like those given by the Americans. Often these arrived in pieces but they still tasted very good to us sweet-starved children.

Auntie Bessie was a fairly formidable lady, in the old 'Schoolma'am' tradition. But she had, as they say, a heart of gold. We knew where we were with her and she was always very good to us children. She wore her hair in a bun and I was always fascinated by its length when she let it down at night. I remember her particularly for her geyser and her dog. The gas geyser heated the water for the bath. It was simple to turn on, but usually, at first, nothing happened. Then after a pause that seemed to last a life time it would ignite with a terrifying explosion. The trouble was that after it was turned on you weren't quite sure when or if it was going to ignite, so you waited in trepidation, and then, just when you had decided it wasn't going to light, there would be this deafening bang.

The dog was a white, stone deaf Staffordshire bull terrier, named Amicus though this was shortened to the more appropriate Cus. He was intelligent, obstinate, enjoyed his freedom and had discovered that it was possible to open the casement windows by the simple expedient of

Cus as seen by me aged twelve

lifting the handles with his nose and pushing. When we visited him and Auntie Bessie, all the handles had been carefully tied up so that he couldn't escape even if he wanted to.

On walks he was kept on a lead. However, on one occasion I remember foolishly letting go of the lead and giving him a shove from behind. This was not a good idea as he set off like a rocket and we only caught up with him again several hours later fortunately none the worse for wear having enjoyed a taste of freedom. Another time we took him for what was to be a circular walk round the streets of Isleworth. We were nearly back at Auntie Bessie's house when Cus decided that he had had enough. He sat down and he resolutely refused to budge. He was a fairly solid animal and in the end we had no option but to return the way we had come - making the walk considerably longer than we would have wished.

Auntie Gladys and Uncle Jimmy were also good friends of my father's. They, too, seemed a little formidable and were very much of the old school. Uncle Jimmy was very good to us as a family. He was Director of Medical Studies at a London Hospital. Both my father and I had cause to be grateful to him, as he undertook to operate on both of us within a space of eighteen months, father for a hernia and me for an appendectomy. Hence we used to joke that Uncle Jimmy knew the Millar family inside out. I can't speak for Father, but I was looked after very well and had royal treatment in the Woolavington Wing for private patients. I was at an age when the ministrations of attractive young nurses were particularly appreciated!

My mother had friends in London too. Auntie Mable and her daughter, Bar, with their respective husbands spring to mind. Bar lived in a cul-de-sac in Strawberry Hill with Digger and their two children who were only slightly younger than Annie and myself. We visited them from time to time. On one occasion I found, in a box of toys, what looked like a rather decrepit air-gun. There were no pellets and I don't think I believed it would work any way. Be that as it may, I put a very tiny stone into the breach and I took it with me round the corner to where the cul-de-sac joined wide main road. Quite soon a horse-drawn milk float came by. It was quite a substantial affair with four wheels and two or more layers of milk bottles. The milkman was sitting up in front driving the horse. In a somewhat desultory way I took aim at the flank of the horse which at that point was about twenty yards away and walking in a sedate manner along the road. I shall never know whether the noise, albeit a fairly insignificant noise, frightened the beast, or whether it was startled by the minute stone which I had placed in the gun. The effect was dramatic. The milk float was last seen heading off into the distance at considerable speed with the milkman hanging on for dear life. Nor did I wait around for further developments. I moved extremely fast back to the house we were visiting, and kept a very low profile for the rest of the day and was relieved when we eventually got home without anything untoward happening.

During the 40s and early 50s we used to take our summer holiday at the beginning of September in Thorpeness, Suffolk. Various friends came with us or visited us. On one occasion our visitors were Uncle Jimmy and Auntie Gladys. If my memory is correct Uncle Jimmy was dressed immaculately in a dark jacket and pin-striped trousers - hardly could it be described as beach wear. At any rate we all wandered down to the beach. Not long after we had sat ourselves down a stray dog of uncertain parentage came snuffling along. Eventually it came across Uncle Jimmy, and whether it had taken exception to his clothes, or had taken a dislike to him for some other reason, it cocked its leg on Uncle Jimmy's pin-striped trousers and ambled off. The older generation were aghast, but the younger ones in the party found it hard to contain their laughter however sorry they felt for Uncle Jimmy.

Our holidays in Thorpeness were great fun. The sea was cold and although the beach was long it was pebbly and extremely uncomfortable to walk on. But Thorpeness did have other attractions. We played lots of tennis at the local Country Club, where entertainment was laid on in the evenings. This included dances on Saturday nights to the music of a local band. During the week there was Bingo, or as it was called then, Housie Housie and scavenger hunts. For these we were given lists of things to collect which varied from centipedes to red flannel underwear. The latter was not something I was familiar with, but I seem to remember that we were pointed in the direction of the Alms Houses and told that they might be a source of such articles of clothing.

Another who came to Thorpeness was Uncle Nick – a pseudo-uncle and a good friend of the family. Two things gave him an aura of mistique. One was that he was divorced and had remarried a young actress. Divorce, of course, was not accepted in the same way as it is today. The other was that he was an actor himself. He appeared on stage and we were later to see him in a number of films. His other claim to fame is that he was the first person to give me a driving lesson. This was not a happy experience. I was wearing gym shoes at the time and my foot slipped off the brake on to the accelerator. Fortunately not too much damage was done. Uncle Nick was very restrained about it, but that was the last driving lesson I had with him.

One of the joys of Thorpeness was the Mere. This was a small lake, only about three feet deep. It was a perfect place for children. At one end was a boat house. In front of this was the main expanse of lake, beyond which were islands and inlets with such evocative names as the Dragon's Lair, and Captain Hooks's Island. This operation was supervised by Albert, the Boatman. He kept a firm, but fatherly eye on things. One of the first times I went on the Mere, I was probably about 16 at the time, he enquired politely if I had sailed before. "Oh yes!" I replied with great self-assurance. So I was allowed to take out one of the small sailing boats. I reached the middle of the lake, but was still in full view of the boathouse when an unfriendly gust of wind caused me to capsize. That was bad enough. To add to my discomfort, as I waded in the muddy water and attempted to right the boat two small boys, probably no more than eight years old, sailed by in an irritatingly confident manner and asked if I needed help. Gritting my teeth, I replied that every thing was fine.

One year when we were on our annual holiday at Thorpeness I was invited to play in a local cricket match. The team was raised by a local landowner, for want of a better expression, to do battle against a team led by Benjamin Britten, who lived and worked in the neighbouring town of Aldeburgh. It was to be played on the Thorpeness village cricket pitch. It was very exciting for me as a teenager, because the opposition contained not only Benjamin Britten but also Peter Pears, whom I caught out at the wicket, and the Earl of Harewood.

The school that I went to following my tree climbing episode and subsequent expulsion was a success. There were three of us boys of a similar age. Most of the other children were girls. I didn't blot my copy book there and in due course I was prepared for Clifton, where I started at the beginning of the Summer Term 1945.

Not too long after I went to Clifton we moved as a family to London. We acquired a large house in Holland Park. At least we called it Holland Park, others might have called it Shepherd's Bush! It was very much where one meets the other. Ours was a pleasant building on a Crescent just off the Bayswater Road. Although we owned the whole building, we only lived in the top flat of four. The next flat down was occupied by an actress and her husband. He at the time was the Stage Manager of The Mousetrap, even then a long running West End stage play. I remember that they lived in extremely cheap accomodation because, as their landlord, my father, was unable to put up their rent owing to the rent act legislation that was in force at the time. Indeed if the communal costs of keeping the exterior of the building and the main staircase in good shape were taken into account I believe we almost paid them to live there!

I only spent holidays in London as I was away at boarding school most of the time. It is not a place that I feel any affinity to. My abiding memory is the smog of 1952. It wasn't like the fogs we occasionally experience today. It was a dirty yellow and seemed to go on for days. Even indoors there was a haze. When it eventually cleared a residue of black dirt was left all round the windows, and all the curtains were so dirty they were immediately taken down and washed. It is no wonder so many with chest ailments died during that period.

Milverton was let while we were in London and on the whole the letting was trouble-free. One tenant did, however, create a problem by digging a ditch from the septic tank in order that it would overflow and the sewage was then diverted to the front path. We could only conjecture that the purpose of this piece of vandalism was so that he could claim the place was unfit to live in and he could therefore withhold his rent. Mercifully, after a short legal battle, the tenant was evicted.

After a few years in London we moved back to Goring. We sold Milverton and bought a large house called The Mount. It sat above the surrounding area adjacent to a cutting through which ran the main London-Bristol railway line. The views across the river, to the Berkshire Downs, were stunning. In the winter months with leaves fallen from the trees it was even possible to spy the river which was only a few hundred yards away, but for much of the year this was hidden by trees and shrubs.

The Mount was situated in two acres of land, which included three tiny little cottages, lawns, a large herbaceous border, a kitchen garden and an orchard, which we subsequently sold for building. Half the main building was converted into two self-contained flats, which were usually occupied by personel from RAF Benson. We had a greater affection for The Mount than for any of our other houses. Two of the cottages were eventually sold as well. In the other there lived an old man. We wanted to modernise this for him: put in a bath, telephone and so on, but he wasn't going to have anything to do with these new-fangled ideas, so the modernisation had to wait until he died. The railway line that ran past The Mount and in those days carried 460 trains every twenty-four hours. Each time a train went past, the house shook. Although some might have found this difficult to live with, in a curious way we found it almost comforting and we very quickly became oblivious to the noise and vibrations! The garden was Father's pride and joy. With guidance from Hilliers he planted numerous shrubs and small trees. He spent many, many happy hours first of all getting the garden the way he wanted it and then keeping it that way. He was still pottering in his garden when, at 85 and now severely handicapped by Parkinson's, my mother instigated the move to a bungalow a few hundred yards away. My father died less than two years later, in 1979. But the new bungalow was to be Mother's home for a further 15 years.

Chapter 4 – Clifton First Time Round

I went to Clifton because my god-father, Albyn Trower was there as a boy. I can't profess to have known him well. But he had been an old friend of my father's. My father and Uncle Albyn were both seriously wounded during the first World War and I suspect that it was while they convalesced that they struck up a friendship. For a while, when I was at Clifton, he was the Referee at Wimbledon. I believe my parents occasionally went to Wimbledon as his guests. I never went during the time he was involved with the Championships, because I was always at school.

For some years I had known that I was entered for Clifton and I had looked forward to taking up my place there. That is not say that I was not apprehensive about it.

I was taken to Bristol by train and shown the House where I was to live for the next two years until I moved to the Senior School. The dormitory that I was to sleep in contained fifteen or more not very comfortable looking beds. Although Clifton is in a major city it is fortunate to be situated in what might be described as a leafy suburb. The dormitory looked out over the Zoological Gardens and more specifically the Polar Bear enclosure. One of the disadvantages of living so close to the zoo was that it was the source of unusual noises. The worst were probably the mating calls of the peacocks. This raucous noise, which tended to occur early in the morning, could in no way be compared with the 'Dawn Chorus'. Another sound was the occasional mighty roar of a lion. I remember one small boy, who had only recently come to the school, being petrified when he heard this noise. It transpired he came from Kenya and thought the lion must be roaming the streets. It took all the skill of the Headmaster's wife to persuade the little chap that the lion was safely locked up.

Other animals, from time to time came to our attention. There were two baby elephants, who used to be exercised in the streets of the area. They were young and mischievous. The keeper who took them for walks didn't always seem to have them under total control. As they walked up a particular tree-lined avenue one of the elephants would lurch into a private garden and help himself to some succulent vegetation. While that was happening the other would head off to another garden in search of some other delicacy. These elephant perambulations soon stopped.

There is a temple in the zoo that is the home of a collection of small bare-bottomed monkeys. On one occasion, during the night, someone thought it would be amusing to put a ladder into the temple and large numbers of the animals escaped and scattered. Some of the residents of the area received rather rude shocks when they looked out of their windows next morning.

In those days it was almost unthinkable to phone home except in dire emergency. I remember a few years later in my final year at school, we heard that there had been a major rail crash on the mainline from London to Scotland at Harrow and Wealdstone Station. Another boy in the house happened to know that his father, the Headmaster of a school in Scotland, was likely to be on that train and was permitted to phone home to find out if his father was safe. In fact he was, and with others, including a restaurant car attendant, he had helped pull the injured out of the wreckage. Some twenty years later this same boy, now a young man, happened to be travelling with his fiancée on the same train. The restaurant car attendant had noticed the name of the young couple and came and asked if they were related to the man who had helped at the scene of the rail crash in 1952. It was of course the same attendant. They had quite a natter!

As I write this, in 2003, phones have to be available in all the boarding houses, and of course, many of the senior school children have mobiles. I made enquiries about these recently and was informed that they are all allowed phones, but they do have to have them switched off during lessons!

So in the 1940s and 1950s letters were virtually the only means of communication between parents and their offspring. I tried, generally successfully, to write home once a week and the weekly letter from my parents was something that was looked forward to with pleasurable anticipation. My first letter, written soon after I arrived at Clifton, was a rather pathetic little effort. I was obviously not very well and had been confined to the 'sickroom'.

My first letter home was a pathetic little offering

May 5th

Pooles
Clifton College
Bristol 8

Dear Mum

I hope you are well. I am awfully unhappy without you and I was crying nearly all yesterday and am crying now because although I am quite popular and have not got into trouble yet I do not like it without you so would you come down before Wednesday. I do not want to make you unhappy but I would like you to come down the telephone number is 34948.

Love to you all
from Colin
I am in bed with a cold.
Now I am up Mummy and am much better.

Transcript of my first letter home

Later letters to my parents were more cheerful though not always very newsworthy, unlike those my parents wrote to me. Almost invariably they started with the sentence, "I hope you are well", and fairly often they concluded with a request for something that I felt I needed.

I consider myself very lucky that I not only enjoyed a variety of sports, but was reasonably proficient at most. On one occasion I was selected to play in five different teams on the same day. I had to choose between Colts rugby, fencing, cross country running, rugby fives and, I think, either boxing or hockey. Cross country running seemed too much like hard work and of the others the sport I had not represented the school at was fives, so that was the one I opted for. I spent almost all of my spare moments indulging in one sport or another and I looked forward with pleasure to the next sporting action. I am sure that this helped make school a much more tolerable experience than it might otherwise have been. I am equally sure that those who were not very athletic, often, but not always, found school less easy to cope with. I believe that today, in 2003, there is much more on offer for the less sporty, which is as it should be. By the same token I am saddened at the lack of facilities and opportunities for sport in the State sector. I am convinced that sport has a part to play in the development of children. Not only is it an important form of recreation, it is also a means of keeping the body fit, of letting off steam and facing physical challenges – surely better than fighting on the terraces at a football match or causing trouble in a city centre on a Saturday night. It can also, I believe, play a useful and significant part in the overall development of young people: introducing the idea of team spirit and working together for mutual benefit and that of self discipline. It is, as well, often a starting point for social recreation and exercise after leaving school.

My most successful sport was probably fencing. I was sorry not to be able to continue with it when I went to University. It was just too expensive at the time. I did represent my college in an inter-college competition, but that was as far as it went. Away matches in any sport were often fun. But fencing against the Royal Naval College at Dartmouth was quite memorable. To begin with we travelled by train. That was a fascinating journey in itself. We also had the whole day off school - another bonus! Then of course we were

I played full back for the 1st XV until I was injured

treated like royalty at Dartmouth College which is set high up above the River Dart in Devon.

I loved rugby fives. The latter to the uninitiated could be likened to playing squash using gloved hands rather than a racket and also using a hard ball. I was also quite reasonable at rugby and played a number of games eventually for the first XV as fullback until I was injured. I played a lot of cricket and was close to being in the First XI. One of my biggest disappointments, when I was at school, was that I didn't quite make the Clifton First XI. In those days Clifton always played against Tonbridge at Lords at the end of the summer term. I would love to have played at Lords! But it was not to be.

One sport I didn't particularly enjoy was swimming. The pool was outdoors and we were expected to swim if the temperature attained the temperature of 58 degrees F - this was not hot! So, especially early in the season, one did not linger in the pool. I could not swim very fast, but could do an acceptable breaststroke, and enjoyed diving, although I was not capable of doing anything fancy. During my two years in the prep school we always bathed in the nude. When it came to the swimming sports, however, it was necessary that we should be more modest as there were a number of spectators present. Few of us had swimming costumes so we were all issued with triangular pieces of material with ties at the side. These sometimes came undone in the middle of a race and in any case only partially did the job for which they were intended!

So for me, School revolved round sport. Work was something that was tolerated. I don't think I was lazy, but I couldn't wait for the next opportunity to get outside and do something energetic. Eventually exams were taken. I did enough at school, as they say, to satisfy the examiners and, after an interview and entry papers for St Edmund Hall, Oxford, I eventually took my place there. I should add that my entry to Oxford was in no small measure due to efforts of my Housemaster, the Reverend Peter Brook. He was a remarkable man. He was a good friend to people of very varied backgrounds. Some of his more shady acquaintances were those he had met on prison visits, whom he had been able to help. Many were grateful for whatever he had done for them. Besides School, rugby, caring for the spiritual needs of the school and prison visiting, one of his main interests was dabbling in Stocks and Shares. After going to Cambridge where he gained a Blue for rugby, he was then capped for England, entered the Church and was an Army Chaplain during the Second World War. He had taken over the House I was in from one, Jock Crawford, a dour Scot who ruled the House with a rod of iron - not unusual in those days. One contemporary some years later put it to me: "Of course you lot never did any thing wrong because you didn't want to upset Peter." For a long time that philosophy worked, although in later years I suspect it didn't hold quite the same power.

Peter always kept his ear very close to the ground, and there is a story of two senior boys, who asked him if they might go to the Memorial Ground to watch a rugby match one evening. Permission, apparently, was refused, but they went anyway. However Peter somehow found out. As he had good rugby connections, he contacted the Memorial Ground and loudspeakers announced to the crowd that there were two boys among them from Clifton

College, who should report to the West Gate where their Housemaster would be waiting for them! Extremely concerned, they hastened off to the West Gate. Their worry was not so much that they had to confront their Housemaster, but that he might elect to send them to the Headmaster. When they met up he pointed out that a School function was due to start in fifteen minutes. If they were back in time he himself would deal with the matter. If they were late it would, of course, become a school matter. The boys encouraged their Housemaster to drive as fast as he could.

I was reminded recently of two other stories about Peter that are worth recording. One concerned two other boys who sought permission to miss the last lesson on a Saturday morning which was the weekly current affairs lecture. They wanted to go to Cardiff to watch the Barbarians against the All Blacks. On this occasion Peter was much more amenable. In fact he was actively encouraging. He told the boys in his usual slow and rather flat tone that he would leave his car unlocked and if they got in it and lay low he would, as soon as he had set some work for his class, come and drive them to Cardiff!

The other occurred when Peter took a dozen or so of us on three boats on the Broads. We had a memorable time. However he did not forget his calling and on the Sunday he decided we should have a Communion Service. He had spotted as a venue a small shed which was probably a fisherman's hut. Someone scrambled through the window and opened up and we assembled inside sitting on piles of rope or whatever else we could find. Peter had brought along his Communion set which he had used during his Chaplain days in the war and so began one of the more unusual services that I have attended.

Peter had children of his own. When it came for me to take my School Certificate I wasn't very well and had to take at least one of the exams from a 'sick room' in the House. It was while I was languishing there that Peter's small twins - they were only two or three years old at the time and very fair - discovered some large tins of sky blue paint intended to redecorate one of the bedrooms. They thought it would be fun to drag the tins along to the bathroom and put them in the bath and then jump in. I didn't actually see them myself, but I do remember the House Matron, who had just seen them, sitting on the stairs, helpless with laughter. Remember this was before the days of emulsion paints so the clean-up process must have posed quite a problem.

Boarding Houses were really run in those days by the Prefects, although they took their tone from the Housemaster. Thus the general ambiance of the House, and I suspect of the school, changed much around this time. When I first arrived at Clifton fagging and beating by prefects were still very acceptable. But over the following years became much less so. I suppose for new boys the Prefects almost appeared like gods. Certainly some showed a bit of swagger as they went about their business. This is well illustrated by the apocryphal story of a head of house who decided he needed to go off to the pub for a drink. Despite warnings and protestations from a friend he set off for the local pub around six o'clock. He walked in only to spy several members of staff already there. Without turning a hair and with great élan he offered them all drinks. They responded with requests for pints and 'doubles'. The head of house drank his pint chatted amiably with the staff and then after half an hour announced that he had to go as he had to be in time to take call-over. No more was heard of the incident.

Memories of school often revolve round the characters that one remembers. My Housemaster was one. Another was a man known as 'Jumper' Gee, who had served in the First World War which he survived with distinction. He volunteered again in 1939 only to be captured in April 1940. He remained a prisoner of war for five years. Eventually he came home to his wife and three daughters, one of whom he had never seen. Despite the hardships involved, he lived to be a hundred, and in his mid 90s was still driving his car in the neighbourhood, though rarely out of second gear! He taught us English and although we used to tempt him with red herrings which he dutifully followed, the fact is he was never dull and we would hang on his every word. A classic comment from him came after one of a series of Lentern services. These took place in the evening in Chapel. That particular year they were taken by an eminent cleric, who went on to become a Bishop of some standing. The future Bishop, like our English teacher, spoke slightly out of the side of his mouth. One morning a bright spark asked our teacher at the start of a lesson what his views on the cleric's address were.

The class could hardly contain themselves when the reply came back that it was all right. "But," he said, "You know he speaks out of the corner of his mouth and people who speak out of the corner of their mouths have warped minds."

The back row of the class used to run a little game - The 'Reputable' team against the 'Disreputable' team. If either of those words were said a goal was scored. Generally the 'Reputable' team won, but occasionally he would get on to the subject of The Miller's Tale or Shakespeare's bed and a string of 'Disreputables' would ensue much to the joy of the back row.

Some of us kept a record of all 'Jumper' Gee's recordable quotes. Once when talking about beauty being in the eye of the beholder he came out with: "One of the most beautiful sights I ever saw was a hole in the road with a pile of drainpipes by it." He also, when discussing Keats' Ode to a Nightingale used to wax lyrical about the nightingales in Nightingale Valley which is just across the river from Clifton.

Rodney Gee was very kind to me and for some reason used occasionally to take me to play cricket for the Gloucester Gypsies, a local nomadic side. He was very keen on his cricket and was a fine opening batsman. Remarkably he was still playing cricket on the Close in his mid sixties.

Another character was the School Marshal. The post of School Marshal was usually ex army and he was responsible for school discipline. But this particular man had just the right blend of discipline, understanding of boys and humour. Every weekday morning he would stand on the steps of the Chapel in a black gown, as boys came in for morning assembly. His main task then was to check that the boys' shoes were clean and that their hair was of a suitable length. This was a busy time. As boys were coming over to Chapel so the girls from the girls' school boarding house were heading up the road to their school. As we didn't see much of girls in those days, the timing of the walk to Chapel was for some quite critical! On one particular occasion the Marshal was chatting to the Chaplain and watching as the first boys started to walk over to Chapel, when he saw that things were not as they ought to be. He turned to the Chaplain and said, "Sir. Look! There's a naked lady over there on the Close."

34

"Don't be silly, Marshal," replied the Chaplain."

But there was, and with that the Marshal, who was fairly portly and not in the first flush of youth, set off in hot pursuit. He eventually caught the lady and covered her modesty with his gown - all this, I suspect, to vocal encouragement of a fairly considerable number of spectators.

The Chapel played a much more prominent part in the lives of pupils in those days. With the exception of the Jewish boys, who had their own House complete with Synagogue, all boys attended

Assembly, was held there six days a week. On Sundays we were always expected to attend the main service of the day and we would sometimes go to an early Communion Service as well. I tried desperately to get into the choir. Somehow I managed it, but I only lasted for about a week as the choirmaster and Director of Music quickly discovered that I was tone deaf.

The Director of Music, Dr Douglas Fox, was another larger than life individual. As a boy he had been an outstanding musician. But in 1914, as his friends went off to war, he felt he could not stay in the safety of Oxford and so he followed them. Then, in 1917, aged just twenty-four, tragedy struck. He was wounded. His right arm was shattered and had to be amputated just below the elbow. Somehow, with help and encouragement from his family and musicians who knew him, he overcame this cruel fate. Despite having only one arm he was still a remarkable organist. Over the years he gave many recitals and those who heard him marvelled at the skill with which he overcame his disability. But it was probably as a teacher of music at Bradfield and then back at Clifton that he really made his name. Like many musicians though he was at times temperamental. The story is told that at one Choral Society practice he became so incensed at what he perceived was the lack of concentration of his singers, that in a fit of frustration, he hurled his gold watch at a boy who caught and returned it. Despite his anger the good Doctor appreciated what the boy had done and gave him £5 - a considerable sum in those days.

Sadly sermons, even the good ones were a turn off for me as I had great difficulty in hearing them. There was one, however, that still stands out in my memory. This was given by a Chaplain in the United States Army, who gloried in the unlikely name of Colonel O Heck. He had a great booming voice, and it was because of this that I heard most of what he said. He preached on the subject of Samson. "Samson," he bellowed, "was the Bible's playboy. He would go up into the hills and he laughed and he laughed and he laughed." By the third "laugh" the Colonel was laughing and so were most of the congregation. He went on to tell us about an amazing machine all covered with inlaid mother of pearl. Then, he asked in his strong American twang, "Does it work - Nope!" And the message - you can't judge things or people by appearances.

Another building that played quite an important part in the lives of the boarders at school was the Sanatorium. The San, which had at least two resident nurses, one of whom had the title of Matron, was where the school doctor held his daily surgeries. If we were unwell we were sent or taken there to be checked out. Surgery was first thing in the morning and if you timed it right you might manage to miss first lesson. However you had to tread carefully when visiting the San, because if the Doctor or more particularly, the Matron, thought you were a little unwell, they would put you off games for a week, and once off games it was very difficult to change the 'sentence' even if there was a very important match coming up! I do remember, however that I had Measles and on recovering from this I picked up Chickenpox. There was a bit of an epidemic, so as there wasn't sufficient room in the San, once we were well enough to get up, we were sent to another building which was adjacent to The Close, the school playing fields. It was spring, the weather was perfect and the only restriction was that we were not to meet up with boys who hadn't had chicken pox. So we spent most of the time out of doors playing football and generally running around.

There were a number of small wards in the san where those who were ill were nursed. One year I had a small operation on my nose and was kept there for some days. If you were really ill it was a good place to be. But convalescence could be extremely boring. On one occasion two or three of us relieved the boredom with a wet flannel fight. Wet flannels were being hurled with gay abandon to and fro. We might have got away with that. Unfortunately the flannel fight spiralled out of control. Then an orange was used as ammunition. As it was flung from one to another, usually missing the intended victim, it hit the walls with a sickening thud and in the process became squashier and squashier. By this time we had already knocked over a small pot containing thermometers, and there were a number of orange 'splodges' on the walls. Next one of the drinking water containers was 'accidentally' emptied on a bed. There was immediate retaliation. Eventually we came to our senses and attempted some sort of clean-up operation. There was also a large damp patch in my bed. When the nurse came in we pre-empted the broken thermometer problem by saying we had had an accident and were very sorry. The smell of orange must have been pretty obvious. We seemed to get off lightly, though I do recall after the nurse had tidied up my bed for me and obviously realized it was damp, she did ask if I was comfortable. Although much embarrassed, I assured her I was.

Eventually my time at Clifton ended. Conscription was still the next step for most boys when they left school. I believe, for many, it provided a wonderful chance to see parts of the world they would not have seen otherwise. However on attending the medical examination I was passed Grade 3 on account of my hearing, and therefore unfit for National Service. So it was decided that I should do a year or two teaching before I went to University.

Chapter 5 – Teaching – The Raw Recruit

The school I went to, Tockington Manor, was typical of many that existed at that time. It had been started by the Headmaster not long after he came out of the army following the end of the Second World War. I arrived straight from school as a young man of 18, was given a class and told, in so many words, to get on with it. Things are very different today. GAP Students, often from overseas, frequently help out in schools, but are neither expected nor allowed to teach. One of the stranger aspects of going straight from pupil to teacher was the fact I was nearer in age to the older pupils than to any of the staff except perhaps for the Assistant Matron, who like me probably came straight from school. So faced with the daunting prospect of my first class for English I simply gave them a dictation - not very original, but it gave me a chance to find out what a class was like and, importantly it ensured the boys were actually doing something. Years later, I found myself mainly teaching the subject that I studied at University namely Geography. But in those early days I taught a variety of subjects.

Once I had taught my first lesson everything became much easier and I soon settled into a routine. However I quickly discovered that teachers have great influence over their pupils and that this could easily be abused. On one occasion I was teaching a class about the growing of tobacco and, in frivolous vein, I told them that cigarettes grew in bunches on trees and that in the spring little men, why little I am uncertain, went round sticking corks on to the flowers in order to produce filter-tipped cigarettes. Tobacco for pipe-smoking was found in holes in trees such as squirrels sometimes use for their nests. Then I proceeded to tell the class how tobacco was really grown. But when I came to give a quick test at the end of the lesson one child had obviously fallen asleep during the latter part of the lesson and in answer to the appropriate question wrote that tobacco was "found in holes in trees."

Every two or three weeks we had to produce grades for effort. If a child got too many minus grades he would be summoned to the Headmaster's study and given four strokes of the cane. What made it worse was the fact that the child would have known what his fate was likely to be well beforehand. Often there was more than one pupil whose grades were below the acceptable level, and they would line up in the dark passage outside the Study door which had a panel of opaque glass. If there were several waiting for punishment to be meted out, those who did not go in first would have to stand outside and listen to the swish and thwack as the cane was administered.

In the cold light of today this seems almost barbaric, but was, I think, not uncommon practice. I suspect some more hardy individuals probably benefited, most children would have shrugged it off as part of life, but I wonder whether it would have had a more lasting effect on a few of the more sensitive souls.

It has to be stressed that I am describing what happened 50 years ago. Corporal punishment is now, of course, outlawed and those who teach in preparatory schools today have a greater awareness of the needs of individual children than they ever did then. Tockington, like any good preparatory school has moved with the times.

Lest those reading this should get the wrong impression I should add that the Headmaster was a warm and friendly man, whose administration of discipline was not out of line with what was common practice in those days. He was very fair and looked after his staff and his pupils well. He was keen on sport of all kinds but particularly cricket. In fact when he was younger he had played for Dorset. He had also been to Clifton as a boy, where like most boys he was not averse to practical jokes. He used to tell a story about himself as a boy.

At the time he was talking about, in the 1920s, staff wore gowns and mortar boards. The master's desk was set at the front of the class on a raised dais. One particular master used to come into the classroom with a great flourish and put his hands firmly on the front edge of the desk, thus often nudging it forward slightly. On this occasion the class arranged the desk so that it was teetering on the very edge of the dais. They also placed piles of exercise books and lots of inkwells - no fountain pens in those days - on the desk and then sat back and waited. On cue the master arrived placed his hands firmly on the desk and the desk, inkwells and books ended in a chaotic heap on the floor. At this point the class, to a boy, leapt to their feet to assist picking

TOCKINGTON MANOR

TERM REPORT

Name _A. Merchant_

LATIN. Set _IV_ No. of Boys in Form _II_ Average Age _10.2_ Place _7_	He has improved considerably during the term and is beginning to think more logically. As a result there is some improvement in his neatness. _G.C.T_
FRENCH. Set _IV_ No. of Boys in Form _II_ Average Age _10.2_ Place _8_	orally not too bad, but written work poor. Badly handicapped by his shocking writing and spelling plus blots! _E.E.B._
MATHEMATICS. Set _IV_ No. of Boys in Form _II_ Average Age _10.2_ Place _2_	He finds the work fairly easy but has yet to learn that neatness & tidiness have some importance. _SB_
ENGLISH. Set _IV_ No. of Boys in Form _II_ Average Age _10.2_ Place _10a_	His grammar is fair; but his spelling and writing are bad. This could be improved considerably if he took greater care. He also needs practice in setting his thoughts on paper. _e.R.Th._
HISTORY. Set _IV_ Place _2nd_	He has tried hard and had good results but again his poor spelling is much in evidence. _e.R.Th._
GEOGRAPHY. Set _IV_ Place _7th_	He has made good progress this term. _e.R._
MUSIC	
DRAWING	fair _N.E.B.T_
GREEK	
GENERAL CONDUCT _Good_ .... rather childish.	A satisfactory start.

Weight at beginning of term   stones   lbs.
     ,,   ,, end   ,,   ,,   ,,   ,,
Next Term begins on **Monday, January 19th.**

               G.C.Tracey

My reports were really rather dull and unimaginative

40

things up. Amid the pandemonium the master concerned retrieved his mortar board. When he left the room, with profuse thanks to all, it was observed that a trickle of Quink blue-black ink was running down his forehead.

Not only did I have to give grades every few weeks, but at the end of term I was expected to write a report for every subject on the pupils I taught. All my reports were written in an exercise book, which was passed to the Headmaster to be checked. I have to confess my reports were really rather dull and unimaginative, unlike one my wife once received which read, "When Gillian grows up her brains will be brand new!"

A year or two ago, at a party, I met up with an ex-pupil, who I know quite well. He produced a copy of his report, much of which I had written. He, at the time was twelve years old, and I was eighteen. The general tone of the report was that he rarely made much effort and was appallingly untidy. This same man is now an eminent Bristol businessman, so my teaching and reports don't seem to have done him much harm!

The school buildings centred round a lovely country mansion and stable block in very beautiful grounds. Unfortunately the main playing fields were situated the other side of a little country road and because the crossing was on a bend it was necessary to see all children across this road. Although children were thus restricted from going to the playing fields unless they could be supervised across the road, there was no such restriction to their playing in the large field situated behind the school. Here, especially in the summer, they could ramble in their spare time whenever they liked, weather permitting. During free time staff wandered round the school buildings and the areas outside to maintain law and order.

There was one room in the stable block called the 'Rag Room'. This was a bare room with windows suitably protected where the boys could kick a small football about without doing any damage except, I suppose, to themselves! It was used a lot, especially when wet, and gave the boys the opportunity to let off steam. On one occasion when I was on duty, I was doing my perambulation through this particular room and was horrified to find a small boy laid out cold on the floor. He was carried upstairs to the sickroom and fortunately soon came round. It was observed that his shoe laces were undone. Like many small boys he rarely walked anywhere when he could run, and in so doing had tripped over his untied shoe laces fallen, banged his head and knocked himself out on the unforgiving floor.

Another time a small boy was seen crying, but surrounded by a sympathetic gathering of friends. It transpired that during lunch a snail had been spotted on his salad. But the boy in question hadn't seen it and of the snail there was no sign, so he drew the obvious conclusion. Eventually after another little boy pointed out that in France they were always eating snails he cheered up.

A duty, even more boring than perambulating round the school was taking the Sunday walk. This involved taking the whole school for a walk, and as I remember it, the absolute minimum length was an hour. The boys would be lined up in pairs and would set off with one member of staff at the front and another at the back. The younger members of staff found this not only tedious, but also testing, because the children didn't enjoy these walks either and inevitably tried to make life more difficult for those in charge by dawdling in some cases, speeding up in others, pushing and shoving each other and so on.

Socialising was not easy in this somewhat cloistered environment. Assistant matrons were a lifeline. If it could be arranged that the matron had a half day that coincided with mine, so much the better. I remember one such matron whose father was a bank manager. She told the lovely story of how her father was posted to Portsmouth. Before the whole family was moved, he went down for a couple of days to meet the staff and generally get his bearings. On the first evening of his stay he thought he would like to go to the theatre. It was early in the year and the only show that appeared to be on was the Pantomine - Babes in the Wood - I believe. So he booked a ticket and later that day took himself off to the theatre only to discover to his horror that he had booked a ticket for a show especially aimed at the large number of naval personnel in the area called My Bare Lady. He felt that for him to be seen going to such a show might not impress future clients. The pantomime only played to matinee audiences. More mature shows filled the evening slot. This same matron also related how her mother ensured her children behaved themselves while her husband and their father was away at the war. Apparently if she was naughty she would be sent to the bottom of the garden to collect one of the canes that supported the carnations. She then had to walk back up the garden with it and hand it to her mother who would use it to make her point. She always maintained the worst part was not the actual receiving of two or three swishes of the cane, but the indignity of having to go and fetch the cane from the bottom of the garden.

On my half day I usually travelled to Bristol, where I could meet a friend, do some shopping and perhaps go to the theatre. Travelling there usually involved a twenty minute walk and then a bus journey of half an hour. If I was lucky I might get a lift with a gentleman who used to visit the school on Thursdays to teach the senior class Greek. This was something of a two-edged sword as he had only one arm and the car was not specially adapted. He had to remove his hand from the steering wheel to the gear lever in order to change gear. As he usually drove at a furious pace I often arrived in Bristol a quivering wreck!

I worked at this school for two years before university and for two after. In between I came back during the latter part of the summer term to help out. One year there was a shortage of space in the main house so one of the ladies who came in daily to help at the school provided me with a room in her home in the village. It was only two or three hundred yards away. The main problem was that the lavatory was in a small shed at the bottom of the garden. Inevitably if I woke up I would wonder if I needed to go. That of course meant that I didn't get to sleep again until I had taken the walk, torch in hand, to the 'outside closet'!

As I have already indicated the regime would be considered strict by modern standards, but it was caring. The busiest time for the matrons was after breakfast. The boys would troop upstairs for their vitamin tablets, cod liver oil or malt extract. They also had to go to the lavatory, to ensure they were 'regular'! After performing they would shout out "Satisfactory" and disappear downstairs. However Matron didn't always trust the children and some were not allowed to flush the toilet so she could check for herself! Those who were not 'Satisfactory' had to return during the day to try again!

There was as with most prep schools a strong emphasis on sport. With small numbers to choose from and consequently a limited number of large pupils, Tockington concentrated on soccer as opposed to rugby. It was felt that with soccer skill had the edge whereas with rugby brawn could predominate.

Matches were very important, probably because if a school was seen to do well at a particular sport it helped sell the school. So every match day, those not involved in the matches were wheeled out to give their vocal support with staff at hand to ensure that the supporters did their job properly. This was a full-time occupation for staff as for some if not most of the onlookers watching others play a match was the last thing they wanted to do. In the summer they could be quietly occupied lying on rugs watching in a desultory way, perhaps digging little holes in the ground, looking for four leaf clovers or scorching leaves with a magnifying glass. Whatever it was, generally it could be done without attracting attention. In the winter it involved standing on the touchline, where it was cold and damp. Chasing someone when no member of staff was immediately at hand was not only fun, but it also helped to keep the circulation going.

One of the highlights of the day for those playing, and for parents who came to see their offspring perform, was the tea. In winter the teams retired to the dining room, but the parents, and staff not supervising the children, were entertained in the Hall. In the summer the boys mingled with the adults on the carefully manicured lawns outside and were able to enjoy tea, cucumber and other types of thinly cut sandwiches, and a mouth-watering array of home-made cakes.

In fact my main winter sport was rugby. As a result of the encouragement of my Housemaster at Clifton I joined the Harlequins. I used to wear a Harlequin jersey sometimes when I took games which gave rise to the nickname I acquired there of Rainbow. Sadly because of school duties on Saturdays I had few opportunities of playing for them. But I do remember playing once against Sherborne School. After the match we had a little time on our hands before the coach returned home. It seemed a good opportunity to visit my god-mother's daughter, Susan, who I knew to be at a neighbouring girls' boarding school. A tentative knock on the door was answered. I was told to wait. The door was left open and numerous young ladies flitted past. I felt like an Adonis. The girls were obviously closeted in the school buildings and rarely saw boys, so the sight of any boy was news. Eventually the lady who had opened the door to me returned and informed me I could take Susan for a short walk round the grounds.

Although I was thrown in at the deep end when I first started teaching I learnt much in those first few years. The Head was very appreciative of the efforts of his staff. He showed this in various ways. If someone organized something well the head would write an appreciative letter and often he would thank them publicly. Also, at the end of some terms he would take all the staff out to dinner or even a show. Every now and then staff would also be invited to drinks in the sitting room. Half days were sacrosanct. Some Headmasters I have served under have not been of the same persuasion. But I remain convinced that half days not only provided an enforced break and rest from daily routine, but if used properly provided the opportunity to see a world outside the narrow confines of school.

Eventually after seven happy years, including the summer terms when at University, I decided it was time to move on. I wanted to see a bit of the world. Initially I had hoped to go to New Zealand, but then a post came up in British Columbia in Canada, for which I was lucky enough to be accepted - but of that more anon.

Chapter 6 – Oxford University

I was very privileged to have had the opportunity to go to Oxford, although I sometimes feel that perhaps I didn't make the most of my time there. Moreover it was almost entirely due to the good offices of my Housemaster, Peter Brook, that I was offered a place at St Edmund Hall. Teddy Hall, as it is affectionately known, was then a small college, situated just off the High Street almost next door to Queen's. My subject was Geography. Very quickly I realised that my poor hearing was a considerable handicap. Unable to hear the lectures I quickly abandoned most of them. I did however persevere with Anthropology lectures which were held in the Pitt Rivers Museum. The lady who lectured us in this subject had obviously travelled widely and the lectures were interesting. She was an authority on the islands of the Far East and, when visiting a primitive tribe of Papua New Guinea, had impressed the Chiefs by her ability to produce appropriate sounds from a "bullroarer". This was, in effect, a thin strip of wood or other available material, about an inch wide and six inches long. It was attached to a piece of string and it was whirled round. This resulted in a booming noise. Much to the delight of the students, the lecturer gave us a demonstration. As she was a tiny individual it was a wonder she didn't take off. Apparently a woman, let alone a white woman, was not expected to be capable of producing sounds from a bullroarer. The local chiefs were most impressed! The Pitt Rivers Museum in those days was a marvellous place. It was crammed from floor to ceiling with artifacts and paraphernalia of every ethnological group you could imagine. There was too much really to take in and it was not set out in an organised way, but it was a veritable Aladdin's Cave. Among this amazing collection were some genuine shrunken heads which had a ghoulish attraction.

Because of my poor hearing I went to lip-reading lessons at the Radcliffe Infirmary. My teacher was a lovely lady, Kathleen Jagger. She commenced work at the Radcliffe Infirmary in 1948 when the government first started issuing free hearing aids. The name of the job, which she created herself, was chosen carefully. She called herself a hearing therapist. The emphasis was on the hearing rather than deafness. She sadly died while I was at University. Equally sadly I don't think I realised how ill she was until almost the end. For a spell I went fairly regularly to see her. I am not sure that she taught me a great deal. I had been deaf for over twenty years by then and had to some extent learned to lip-read, albeit sub-consciously. But I enjoyed going to visit her. We had long chats about all sorts of things. It seems that many partially deaf people find their affliction quite difficult to cope with. This is partly because deaf people so often don't appear to have anything wrong with them, and so very few people make allowances for the fact that they are deaf. Deafness seems to arouse less sympathy than other comparable afflictions. Also because they don't hear or are struggling to hear what has been said they often react slowly. Consequently others sometimes label them as mentally slow or at worst stupid. Yet they themselves can feel very cut off from other people, who so often don't see the need to treat them any differently from anyone else. Too often they say, "He can hear when he wants to," and put half the trouble down to obstinacy, without realizing that even if there was some substance in this, hearing requires such a terrible effort of concentration and apparent inattention is simply a much needed rest. I understood from Miss Jagger that Lester Piggott was one of her patients. She told me what the world knows now, but perhaps didn't appreciate then, that Lester was deaf and that was probably a major reason why he sometimes appeared so surly.

Given my hearing impairment, it may seem strange that I should want to teach. I find greatest difficulty hearing in large auditoriums and churches. Being in a large room, where people are scattered is never easy either. Curiously in a crowded room in a cocktail party situation, I never find it particularly difficult. I sometimes wonder if, in those circumstances, I am able to cope better than most people that have good hearing. There is no doubt ability to lip-read a little helps in this situation.

In the classroom I tended to move around as much as possible. I wore my hearing aid much of the time. If I wasn't wearing it and I found myself struggling I would be quite open about it and say, "I can't hear you. I must get my ear trumpet out." If children mumbled or spoke with their hands over their mouths I would tell them to speak more clearly or take their hands away from their mouths. Although such openness wasn't always easy, on the whole the children respected this approach. I don't ever remember feeling that children were making fun of me or taking advantage of my disability.

Many years later when I was Acting Headmaster I had a small hearing aid which fits in the ear, purchased at great expense. Sadly it fell out of the little box in which I kept it. Unfortunately there was a tiny hole in my pocket - just big enough to allow a small hearing aid to pass through! At Assembly, the day after I discovered the loss, I offered a reward to anyone who found it. A little while later a boy arrived at my study saying, "I think I have found your hearing aid, Sir." With that he produced a small mass of mangled wires and plastic. Sure enough it was the aid but regrettably someone had inadvertently stepped on it. The child was duly rewarded, but the hearing aid was never going to be quite the same again! I contacted the insurance company, who sent an assessor to see the damage and to check up on what perhaps seemed to them an unlikely story.

Perhaps I should add that recent technology and particularly the loop system that is to be found in most theatres, churches and other public buildings has made an enormous difference. I remember the first time I switched into it in the Clifton Chapel. A young Welsh girl read from the pulpit at the School Carol Service. I can't recall the actual reading. But I do remember she read beautifully. I heard every word and was completely mesmerized.

So at Oxford where such facilities did not then exist I depended very much on tutorials and I didn't always find these easy from a hearing point of view. They were usually held once a week. A topic to discuss would be given and some references that we could look up, and then we were told to go off and research the subject and write an essay. One of the advantages of studying at Oxford was having access to one of the world's great libraries. Because I didn't go to lectures I was very conscientious about writing these essays and set myself the target of working seven or eight hours a day. At the end of a week the tutorial group would return to the tutor. One or more of us would read our essays and then we would discuss the topic. Early on I set out to impress a particular tutor whose subject was Anthropology – not the one of "bullroarer" fame. I wrote an essay of some 24 pages of A4. At the following tutorial I started to read my magnum opus. Very quickly the tutor's eyes glazed over. We didn't even complete page one! "Get the attention of the listener," he said." Start with an anecdote and never write more than eight pages!" Thereafter my first aim was always to find a suitable story with which to start the essay.

Oxford is probably at its best in late spring. To visit the Parks at this time must be high on the list of the pleasures of being at Oxford. There was nothing more pleasant than to wander through the Parks on a warm May afternoon. If so inclined one could pause to take in a cricket match between the University and a visiting County side. The Parks was not always so peaceful. I have wandered through in the winter months only to be almost trapped by a horde of rather Amazonian lady lacrosse players - or so they seemed to me at the time. The reason for this is that lacrosse unlike most sports has no boundaries. The Parks in the spring and early summer takes some beating though. In May, and June too, the Cherwell beckons. This small tributary of the Thames forms one boundary

But now I had a degree

of the Parks. There is a little footbridge over it that reputedly is the original site of the bridge where Pooh and his Friends played Poohsticks. For those who are unfamiliar with Winnie the Pooh, Poohsticks is the game where sticks are dropped one side of the bridge with a view to seeing which stick appears on the other side first.

The Cherwell is a favourite punting river, where students can spend a few relaxing hours. If you travel upstream from Magdalen Bridge you passed, on one side, Parson's Pleasure an area set aside for male dons to sunbathe and swim unclothed. Ladies were not supposed to pass along this stretch of river, but were expected to disembark and walk round the area before re-embarking again on the other side. More often than not, they simply lay down in the bottom of the punt, covered over with rugs, and may be even, if they dared, have peeped out from under the rug to view what, I suspect, was not a very edifying sight!

The summer was the time for cricket. I was lucky enough to play an enormous amount - even in my last term. Once or twice I had as many as six games organised in a week, although occasionally, perhaps fortunately, games were rained off. I kept wicket so was involved for much of the time. Games often started at 11 am and went on with suitable intervals for lunch and tea, till 6.30 pm. This meant that I had to discipline myself to get in two or three hours work before a game and then four or five in the evening which took me well into the night.

Three years passed very quickly, and in no time I was back teaching at the school where I had started my teaching career, but now I had a degree and could command an improved salary. I was to stay at that school for a further two years before eventually spreading my wings and going further afield.

Chapter 7 – Across Sea and Land

Having put in an application for the post in British Columbia, I was thrilled when I received the invitation to meet the Headmaster of the school for an interview. He was coming to London and would I meet him there in a small hotel somewhere in the West End. The meeting duly took place. The job sounded very exciting. Chuck Curtis, in fact, was English and had worked at Shawnigan Lake, a well-known Canadian independent school run along English Public School lines, for a number of years. He wanted to set up a school of his own for children in Grades up to and including seven. At the same time Shawnigan Lake would shed some of the lower grades and concentrate on the older children. The school was to be modelled on the English Preparatory School. It was to be on the edge of Shawnigan Lake on Vancouver Island, which is on the Western side of Canada. Chuck was looking for young staff with just a little experience and plenty of energy to help him get started. After the interview there was a wait. I heard nothing for weeks. Even months went by and still nothing. Eventually I received the letter I had been hoping for. I had been offered the post. The long delay had been due the fact that my new Headmaster had had a heart attack - not perhaps a good omen! At last I could set about planning my journey by sea and land to Shawnigan Lake, which was to become my home, not for two years as I had intended, but four.

My parents took me down to Southampton and then came on board to look over the ship, on which I was to travel to Canada. It was called the Batory. With the prospect of at least two years away, it was an emotional strain for all of us. I didn't want them to leave and yet I knew the lingering "Good-bye" was making things worse for all of us. Eventually I suggested that they ought to go as I should go and sort myself out. Once they had gone I felt better and I was able to explore the ship properly.

This was August 1959 and the Cold War was still very much a fact of life. Ten years earlier the Batory's crew had befriended a communist who had jumped bail from the American courts. As a result of this and further newsworthy incidents she was, in 1951, blackballed by the Port of New York and transferred to the Gdynia – Bombay – Karachi service. By 1959, however, she was back on the North Atlantic run carrying large numbers of middle-aged East Europeans who, somehow, had obtained permission to travel to meet up with relatives in Canada and presumably other parts of North America.

I was among a small group, seven or eight, of English-speaking passengers, all in their early twenties. We had the time of our lives. The crew, and particularly the Chief Steward, indulged us despite our attempts to disrupt the smooth routine of the ship. I suspect we provided a welcome relief from the normal somewhat boring schedule. One of a number of escapades involved the swapping round of a number of signs that read Panie and Panowie, Polish I believe, for Ladies and Gentlemen. We thought it hugely funny at the time though with hindsight it seems pretty puerile. The officers however remained friendly and even organised a party for us one night. Eventually we sighted Newfoundland, the most Eastern part of Canada. But we were still a day or two from our destination and that included a stop in Quebec. From Quebec we sailed on up the St Lawrence. The outstanding feature of that part of the journey that still stands out nearly fifty years on was the large number of sawmills and piles of logs and wood chips that lined the bank.

The night before our eventual landfall our small group met to discuss how we could stamp our impression on the voyage. Eventually it was decided that one of our number should climb up the main mast and pin some memento to the masthead. So it was, at about one o'clock in the morning, just before we arrived in Montreal, that one of our group, carrying a pair of red knickers sacrificed by one of the girls shinned up the mast and fix the garment so that it fluttered proudly from its position above the ship. After completing this operation we retired to our cabins, perhaps just mildly apprehensive that we were about to spark an international incident. After all it was a Communist ship. However sleep soon enveloped us. Next morning there was great activity as the ship docked in Montreal. We quickly went on deck so to observe our handiwork of the night before. But when we looked up at the main mast there was no sign of the red knickers. Eventually we disembarked and were standing on the quayside exchanging addresses and bidding fond farewells when the Chief Steward wandered up to the group. We were quick to tell him how much we appreciated what he and some of his fellow officers had done to make our journey so special. Then he said in broken English, "Ah yes. Zee Red Pantalons! Zey belong to you!" and he nodded at one of the girls in the group! There were obviously no hard feelings.

So we scattered in different directions. My journey continued by train. Two great railway lines the Canadian Pacific and the Canadian National stretched from one side of the country to the other, across five time zones. The size of this country is hard to comprehend to those of us who have lived most of our lives in a small country like England. The journey took three or four days and nights. The train crawled across this immense land. From Montreal we skirted immense lakes, which are more like inland seas. On the side of the train away from the lakes were huge rocky outcrops and vast wildernesses of coniferous forest. We passed through exciting cities and towns on the way west. There was Sudbury with its colossal nickel quarries. Then there were the twin lakehead cities of Port Arthur and Fort William, now merged into one named Thunder Bay. Originally there were two cities, each with its ranks of grain elevators as the two railway lines were in hot competition and each had to have its outlet to the lakes through which vast quantities of grain were shipped to Britain and other countries in Europe. The two railways came close together again at Winnipeg as they were channelled between the American Border and Lake Winnipeg. So the train chugged on across the Prairies, mile after mile of open country, with only the occasional farmstead and every now and then a couple of grain elevators standing sentinel by the railroad. So it moved on to Calgary, the home of the Stampede, the best known rodeo in the world. Soon after leaving Calgary the train started its tortuous journey through the Rockies, at one stage climbing by way of tunnels in great loops so that the front of the train was actually above the rear. After the snow-capped peaks of the Rockies we then crossed the great Okanagan Valley with it thousands of acres of fruit trees. Eventually the train emerged through more mountains into the Fraser delta and Vancouver. What a spectacular city this is with its backdrop of mountains and island-studded sea in front. But even now the journey wasn't ended. There was still the ferry crossing to Vancouver Island, surely one of the most spectacular ferry journeys in the world. Finally after a road journey of some thirty or forty miles I reached my destination, Cliffside Preparatory School.

Cliffside was a collection of white painted wooden buildings

To reach Cliffside it is necessary to turn left off the Island Highway and head through the forests to the village of Shawnigan, which consisted of a main general store, a hardware store, a beauty salon, a garage, a coffee shop and a few scattered houses. At the crossroads where this muster of buildings was sited it is necessary to turn left again and then to follow the edge of the lake for three or four miles. There were a number of holiday cabins along the way, and about a half of a mile from Cliffside there was an old Canadian Pacific Hotel, set fifty feet or more above the lake actually on the railway line. At this time it had been converted into a girls' boarding school. One or two trains a day still passed along the line. The Dayliner, as I believe it used to be called, made one journey up the island and back again each day. If you wanted the train to stop, you simply walked from the room that was used as the staff room on to the platform with a red flag and waved it. There was also the occasional logging train carrying logs to a collecting point on the coast. Here the logs would be made into great floating rafts and dragged by a small tug to a timber or pulp mill from whence they would be made into pulp and then eventually paper. As the trains crossed many unprotected level crossings they would announce their arrival with very loud blasts on their horns and the ringing of bells. They could be heard for miles.

Cliffside was a collection of white painted wooden buildings that I understand, had been the summer residence of a judge. They weren't the most substantial buildings, but they were a start. When I arrived that August afternoon in 1959 it was hard to imagine a more beautiful spot. The buildings nestled at the foot of a mountain. Beyond the buildings was the lake itself, perhaps half a mile wide at that point, and some four miles long. On the other side of the road along which we had just travelled was an area which a year later we bulldozed into a playing field. Then beyond that the mountain rose steeply to a summit that was a thousand feet above the lake.

We swept in through the entrance down towards the lakeside. There was a group of willing hands working away to get things ready for the opening. I quickly found myself occupied. I was given a hacksaw - my first job to cut horizontally a consignment of bunk beds that had been acquired from a logging camp so that they could be used as single beds! The next project was to create a small building to house the school medical centre.

This beautiful spot was to be my home for at least the next two years. I couldn't believe my luck. I am sure that if you are away from parents and relations for any length of time friendships that you make become particularly close as a way of making up for the absence of family. Certainly I found this true.

That wasn't to say that my family, and particularly my parents, weren't very much in my mind. The weekly letter that I received from my mother was something that I always looked forward to. Most of my new friends were people who worked at the three private schools situated on the lake. At the north end was Shawnigan, a senior boys' school. Less than half a mile from us on the same side of the lake as us was Strathcona girls' school and then there was Cliffside.

My parents visited me while I was in Canada, of which more anon, and I did return home for two or three weeks for my sister, Ann's, wedding in 1960. She was married in the lovely old church of St Bartholomew the Great, which is just next to St Bartholomew's Hospital in the City of London. She was married there because it was a church we had attended quite often during our spell in London. As well as being old - it was begun in 1123 - and a very beautiful church, the choir, so I was led to believe, was made up, at any rate in part, of singers from Covent Garden. There was, however a little problem. At that time, in order to be married in a church you generally

The next project was to create a small building to
house the school medical centre

56

had to have resided in that parish for a period immediately prior to the wedding. Of course thousands of people work in the City, but very few live there. Ann actually had to pack a bag and leave it with the vicar for three weeks so she could claim residence!

My return to Canada after the wedding was not entirely straightforward. I had booked a flight via Amsterdam and decided while there to see a little of the city. I had most of the day to visit the Rijksmuseum and explore some of the waterways, and the old parts of the city before returning to Schipol, Amsterdam's main airport, for the on-going flight to Vancouver. But the flight was delayed. Eventually we were bussed to a local hotel for what was to be a fairly short night. I was asked if I would mind sharing a room with another male passenger. Naively I agreed. Subsequently I discovered that I had to share a double bed with this complete stranger. The night couldn't be short enough. I spent the whole of it teetering on the edge of my side of the bed, and didn't really relax again until dawn broke and we were summonsed to breakfast before continuing on our way.

Chapter 8 - Canada

Because of the relative remoteness of the school, and indeed, of the area generally, one of my first requirements was a car. Up to that point, I had driven very little so the day I went to take delivery of the second-hand Volkswagen Beetle with a sunshine roof was quite an experience. The sunshine roof was not a requirement that day as it was pouring with rain, so much so that I could hardly see where I was going and in those conditions I wasn't feeling very happy about driving the car anyway. A year later I was able to purchase my first new car - a brand new green Sunbeam Alpine convertible. It was fast and it had a lovely throaty roar so that it sounded fast as well! The only drawback was that if I came home late people along the lake-side road would hear it and know it was me! Several times I was confronted with comments like, "Colin, you were late last night!"

Following my arrival at Cliffside in August 1959 I spent the next few weeks working hard with other staff and friends of the Headmaster trying to get the place clean and welcoming for the first pupils. There were, if my memory

It was fast and it had a throaty roar

58

serves me right, less than twenty to start with. By the end of the first year that had crept up to about forty and by the time I left there were nearly 70 pupils. With the increase in numbers of pupils so the staff numbers increased. Initially beside the Head and myself there was another Englishman, who, like me, had been appointed following an interview in England. There were a couple of other locally recruited teachers and Jim and Hilda. The latter were a couple from Yorkshire, but they had been in Canada for a few years. When Jim first joined the staff he was still looking after a herd of dairy cattle a few miles away, but in due course he became the school's full time handy man and general factotum. Hilda was the matron and looked after the health and general well-being of the children. There was also a Chinese cook, Mr Wong, and a chaplain, who was really attached to Shawnigan Lake School, but helped out on a part time basis.

We always seemed to have Chinese cooks and so our food had a somewhat Chinese flavour. There were large numbers of Chinese on the west coast of Canada. One New Year's Eve the two newly-arrived English staff were invited by Mr and Mrs Wong to the home of one of the Chinese community in Duncan, a small town a few miles further north, to celebrate the occasion. We felt very honoured, as we were the only non-Chinese there. I don't remember what we ate, except that there was besides fish an amazing array of dishes and we all helped ourselves to what we wanted with our eating utensils, chopsticks. After the meal a small group settled down to play Majong. This is a game played a lot by the Chinese and that evening dollar bills of various denominations seemed to be exchanging hands with great regularity. This didn't altogether surprise us as when Mrs Wong had her day off, a Tuesday, she used to go off to Victoria, the capital city of British Columbia, with a view to seeing if she could increase the value of her pay cheque. She usually did. Occasionally we would invest $10 in her Majong skills!

It was to Duncan that I took myself one day when I decided I should become a true Canadian. I elected to have a crew cut. It is extraordinary what the removal of one's hair can do to one's appearance. I came out of the barber's and spotted Jim and Hilda on the other side of the road. I shouted to them but to begin with they totally ignored me! It was only after persistently

I elected to have a crew cut

shouting, "It's me! It's me," that they recognised me.

The school originally included two dormitory blocks, single storey wooden buildings. Each housed ten or twelve boys and was heated with one oil stove. We named these after Coastal Indian tribes. Mine was called Haida. This West coast tribe was renowned particularly for the magnificent totem poles that they carved. There was also the main classroom block, with a chapel on the top floor, and the dining block as well as one or two other buildings including the water tower and the boathouses. The water tower was situated at the highest point of the property and had on the top floor (of two) a huge wooden tank in which our water was stored. On the outside of the building was a pointer that moved up and down as the level of water in the tank went up and down. All our water, including that used for drinking was pumped directly from the lake. It was checked fairly regularly by local health officials. A year or so after the opening of the school a purpose built dormitory block was built.

The two boathouses, which housed one or two small boats and later on a large Indian canoe, were of the floating variety, and the boys used to swim from them. Those who couldn't swim wore lifejackets. Those who could swim had to do so with a 'buddy' so that, should they get into difficulties, there was someone to help them and raise the alarm. They were of course carefully supervised. You can't be too careful where water is concerned. This was brought home to me very forcefully when one child thought it would be amusing to tie a large rock to his feet. As it happened the rock was so heavy that he was not strong enough to keep himself afloat. Fortunately

Much of the PE was done outside

he was spotted promptly and dragged back on to the pontoon gasping for air, but apart from that none the worse for wear.

Many years later, I was swimming in the pool at Clifton, still an outdoor pool at the time, with a group of adult friends. There was a lot of laughter and everyone was enjoying themselves. Suddenly it dawned on us that one of the girls was in difficulty. She was dragged to the side of the pool, and soon recovered. But the incident, like the one at Cliffside, was a salutory reminder of how easy it is for accidents to happen in a pool, let alone a lake, particularly if no-one is on what one might call 'lifeguard' duty.

I taught English, Maths, and Humanities, which was Canadian for History and Geography. After the freedom of teaching in an English Prep School I found the constrictions of teaching in a Canadian school a shock to begin with. The Provincial education department laid down very clear guidelines as to what should be taught and what text books should be used. The reason for this is that it was thought important that all children of a given year group in the province should be learning the same thing. To get such uniformity over such a large area it was necessary to have very clear cut guide lines. So children who were in small isolated settlements up near the Arctic Circle would be covering the same work as those in large schools in metropolitan Vancouver. As well as academic subjects I took the children for PE and games which included cricket and rugby. Much of the PE was done outside. But when the weather was unsuitable we took them in the minibus to the gym at Strathcona.

It was when returning from there that I had a very lucky escape. I should explain that the road which connected the two schools was narrow and winding, and ran round the edge of the lake. There was a speed limit of something like fifteen or twenty mph. It had been raining cats and dogs for the previous twenty-four hours. The minibus was full of boys and we were travelling very slowly. Because of the large amount of surface water it was impossible to see where the hard surface ended and the soft shoulder began. Suddenly the offside wheel began to sink into the rain-sodden shoulder. Inexorably the minibus rolled over and down the small embankment, ending upside down in the shallow waters at the edge of the lake. I turned off the ignition, checked that the boys were all right and told them to scramble out as best they could. It had all happened in slow motion and all the boys except one put their hands out to protect themselves. The one had slight concussion and spent a night in hospital as a precaution. The boys were abuzz with excitement. I was relieved, but it wasn't till I went to bed that the enormity of what had happened dawned on me and I thought how dreadful the consequences of that accident might have been. Sleep did not come easily to me that night. It is a good thing we don't know what is ahead of us!

Another incident, which could well have had worse consequences, occurred one Hallowe'en Night. The children were given a small number of fireworks to set off with very strict instructions about how they should be lit. One boy, contrary to all instructions, thought it would be interesting to light one of these small 'bangers' and put it down a pipe that he found lying around. Then he looked down the pipe! He was rushed to hospital, but was very fortunate not to suffer any permanent damage.

Despite this last anecdote, it has always been my opinion that children have a sense of self preservation within them. It worries me that more and more we wrap our children in cotton wool. They are accompanied everywhere. And, of course, nowadays if there is an accident someone always has to be blamed and the school or whoever is deemed responsible is sued for large amounts of money or worse. Be that as it may it was the school's policy, and it became mine when I ran a school boarding house in an English school some years later, to allow the children to wander off provided they were accompanied by at least one other child and I knew where they were going. Having said that at Cliffside there wasn't very far to go. Occasionally boys would hike up Mount Baldy, immediately behind the school. I always felt it was somewhat ironic that the only time anyone got hurt doing this climb was when we supervised a large group and a rock dislodged by one of the leaders bounced down the mountainside and struck one of the backmarkers. Fortunately the damage was fairly superficial.

Very early on in that first year the Headmaster had another heart attack. It was serious. I remember visiting him in hospital. I am not very good in hospitals as I have a tendency to pass out! I took one look at his grey, strained face and decided it was time for me to leave! The period while he was away from the school was difficult. But we survived and eventually after two or three months the Head made a very welcome return.

Of course Canada was different in so many ways. One mistake that some English people make is to think that because Canadians in the English-speaking part of Canada speak a similar language they are just the same as us. In France, for example, because the language is different allowances are made for the different culture. In Canada and certainly in Western Canada, because of the similarity of language it is more difficult to make those allowances for other differences. In fact, of course, even the language has variations in pronunciation and inflection and a few words are different too. For example petrol, boot and pavement are gas, trunk and sidewalk. Certainly no well brought up young man would ask a girl if she would like a knock up even if you are playing tennis. I also was for ever being teased about my pronunciation of bath with a long 'a'.

Canada is vast and because it is so large, huge areas of it contain very few people. You could fit six United Kingdoms into British Columbia alone and yet in 1959 well under two million lived in the province. When I was there it was suggested that it might be possible to go to Montreal meet a friend coming from the UK and visiting the West Coast of Canada. In fact Montreal is a little nearer Vancouver than London, but not by very much. Nova Scotia on the Eastern Seaboard is certainly nearer to Ireland than it is to Vancouver. Another indication of the size of Canada is that Vancouver Island, that tiny speck that shows up off the west coast on most maps of Canada, is the size of Wales and Northern Island put together. The immense area of Canada is perhaps emphasized by the fact that the country is spanned by five or six Time Zones. Newfoundland on the east coast is 3 hours behind Greenwich. British Columbia is eight behind. But it isn't as simple as that. Whole provinces were not necessarily covered by a single time zone. To confuse even more some provinces, in those days, introduced daylight saving time (the equivalent of BST) and others didn't. There was one further complication and that was that all train stations showed Standard Time and not Daylight Saving Time even if the latter was in operation in that area. It is a wonder anyone ever caught their trains! Or maybe they always got there too early!

Every year on 1st January the American Universities have their 'Local Derby' Football Matches – a bit like the Varsity Match. One year I went round to the house of a friend, who like me was keen on football - American Football. Most, if not all the matches were televised. The first would appear on the TV screens in British Columbia at around 10.00 am. As the day progressed so matches further West would start, until eventually those on the West Coast began. By that time those that started in the morning had finished. So we sat, glued to our TV sets switching from channel to channel, with occasional cups of coffee and sandwiches, from ten o'clock in the morning till late afternoon.

Because of the size of Canada distances did not have quite the same meaning as in this country. I remember receiving a phone call at ten o'clock one evening. A colleague phoned, "Could someone please pick me up from the Ferry?" Without thinking, I was on my way although it involved a round trip of 100 miles.

Another feature of travelling in this part of the world was that if the journey necessitated getting to the mainland a ferry trip was involved. The ferries were quick and efficient. Pre-booking wasn't necessary. As I said earlier the ferry journeys off the coast of BC were spectacular. The quickest took just under two hours.

I remember returning one New Year's Eve. This time on a ferry that took a little longer and docked at Nanaimo, a town some fifty miles north of Cliffside. Just as I got off the ferry I encountered a road block that had been set up by the RCMP – not on horseback, but certainly wearing traditional headgear. They were breathalysing motorists, but the method was fairly crude. When I wound down the window the policeman stuck his head through it and took a deep breath. I was deemed not to have been drinking!

Occasionally we had to travel to Vancouver for matches, which was always an exciting day out for the children. One particularly memorable occasion was during the Cuban Missile Crisis when there was a stand off between the Russians and the Americans. It was one of those perfect days - not a cloud in the sky. But we were very aware of the dark storm clouds on the international horizon, particularly as Vancouver was an important seaport and not far from naval bases in Victoria and Seattle.

The other reason for remembering this day was that we went to Vancouver to play a cricket match. Teaching Canadians and Americans to play cricket had proved difficult if not impossible. On this particular occasion we were batting and a very thickset young man of thirteen going on twenty came in to bat for us. He struck his first ball a powerful blow, not perhaps an orthodox drive, more a full-bloodied baseball shot. The ball disappeared into the distance with which the batsman set off at great speed towards cover point. Pandemonium broke out as the fielding side realised they might have a chance to run out this powerful striker of the ball and the batting side were shouting instructions to their man to head for the other end. Suffice to say that the batsman survived, but didn't achieve the number of runs that he might have done if he had plotted a more accurate course.

As will be obvious I have always had a passion for all kinds of sport. As well as American Football (and Canadian Football which was very similar),

I enjoyed watching Hockey (Ice Hockey). To begin with I couldn't cope with the aggression and fights that all seemed part of the game. It appeared all so unsporting. I soon got over these qualms! With friends I used to go quite often to Victoria to watch the Victoria Cougars playing. But every Saturday night National Hockey League games were televised, sponsored by Esso. 'Saturday Night was Hockey Night'. Whenever possible, a group of us including Jim & Hilda, gathered round a television set to watch among others, legends like Frank Mahovolich and Gordie Howe playing for such teams as the Toronto Maple Leafs and the Chicago Black Hawks. I never did quite get to grips with baseball, or basketball. Of these the former seemed just a glorified form of rounders and, while I overcame my distaste for some of the less sporting aspects of Hockey, I was never happy about the arguing that seemed to go on between the players and the arbiters of baseball games. Lacrosse, which is, in fact, the national sport of Canada, I sadly never actually saw being played.

Much of Vancouver Island was covered with coniferous forest and because of this there was a constant alertness for the dangers of Forest Fires. It was not uncommon to see in huge letters on major roads, "KEEP BC GREEN USE YOUR ASH TRAY". The first summer after I arrived I looked for a job during the summer vacation. I applied for and was offered a post as the Foreman of a Fire Suppression Crew. This would have involved being in a remote area of forest and keeping a lookout for forest fires. If a fire started in my area I would alert the authorities and then, with my team, I would have to help fight it. Unfortunately, at the last moment the Head changed the date of the end of the summer term and I was unable to take up the post. Occasionally in a bad year several hundred fires might be burning at the same time. To give an example, in July 1963 there was a report in the local press stating that 373 fires were burning in different parts of British Columbia. These are sometimes started by lightning strikes. When that is the case they may be in a very inaccessible places. One of the Forestry Department's weapons for fighting such fires was the huge Martin Mars flying boat. These massive planes were adapted to swoop down on a lake near the fire scoop up something in the region of 6000 gallons of water and then dump it on the fire. Other fires are started as a result of careless acts - cigarette thrown away thoughtlessly, or a camp fire not put out properly.

One summer two young boys climbed to the top of Mount Baldy, the mountain just behind Cliffside. When they reached the top they lit a small fire that they knew their parents would be able to see from their house across the lake, to show them that they had reached the summit. Unfortunately the fire got out of control and the emergency services were called in. The two boys were made to pay for their carelessness. Every time another shovel or some other item of equipment was needed they were sent down the mountain to collect it.

Fire practices were held regularly and were taken very seriously. I remember one evening while we were having rugby training at a local school gym we received a call to help as there was a house fire just down the road. By the time we reached the fire, and it did not take us long to get there, every single part of the building was alight. There was nothing that we could do except stand and watch as the building was consumed by the flames. Within a very short while all that was left was a pile of smoking ash and a chimney stack. Fortunately no one was hurt, but it was a numbing experience and a powerful illustration of how vulnerable the typical, wooden house of western Canada was to fire. So fire practices were taken seriously, but they didn't always go according to plan. They had one at the girls' school down the road around ten or eleven o'clock one night. This building was three or four stories high and the practice involved climbing down ladders at the rear of the building. For safety's sake young firemen were stationed at the foot of the ladders. The girls, some in their curlers, were duly roused, and started to clamber down until they spied the men at the bottom of the ladders, at which point they turned tail, and amid screams of horror, retreated back to their rooms. That was the end of that particular fire practice.

Many of the staff at Strathcona were very good friends and, when my parents decided to visit me, it was they who helped find a small cabin just in front of their school, where mother and father could stay. It was an idyllic spot very close to the edge of the lake. They had come out to Canada on a small cargo ship, which had room for a few passengers, and had travelled through the Panama and up the west coast of North America, a journey I was to do a year or two later in reverse. When I was busy at school they would potter about. There was a small boat that went with the cabin and Father tried his hand at catching trout, but without success. People were rarely to be seen walking in Canada as distances were so great. But my parents were frequently observed striding out along the road to the village and this hadn't gone unnoticed. On one occasion Father let it be known at the village store that he had been trying unsuccessfully to catch trout in the lake. Then one day they returned from an outing and there, hanging up under the eaves of the verandah, were a couple of trout that the owner of the village store had left for them.

Chapter 9 – Canada at Large

This was an exciting time in my life. I had few responsibilities, my job was fun and there was nothing like the same amount of paperwork that is associated with teaching today in England. The holidays too were often very enjoyable.

The very first Christmas I had in Canada, a group of us including some of the staff from Strathcona, the girls' school just down the road, set off for a ski holiday to Banff in the heart of the Rockies. Summer or winter, this is a lovely area. I remember vividly our first night. It was Christmas Eve. For most of us it was the first time we had spent Christmas away from home and we were thousands of miles away. All of us were very homesick and miserable. We missed our families enormously. However next day, Christmas Day, dawned bright and sunny. Soon we were on the slopes of this beautiful skiing area and the blues of the night before were blown away as we hurtled down the piste.

One of the attractions of Banff are the sulphur springs. Wallowing in these pools, which were out of doors, was a curious sensation. The air temperature might be -10° F and the smell of sulphur was strong. But a water temperature of well over 100° F made them an attractive place to soak our weary limbs after a hard day's skiing.

The summer holidays were long. Two summers I spent working in a small family hotel on the other side of the lake. The waitresses were nearly all students from the University of British Columbia. Also employed by the hotel was a young fellow, who owned a boat, which he used to give the guests from the hotel water skiing sessions from the hotel pontoon. He would also take the staff out when he wasn't too busy. Inevitably with such a gathering of youngsters there was a certain amount of high jinks. One night we raided the Girls' dormitory which was in the attic of the hotel and had a beer or two before disappearing into the night again. In fact acquiring the beer in British Columbia at that time was not easy as those under 21 were not able to buy, or even allowed to drink, alcohol. It was also a serious offence to have in your car an opened bottle of wine or spirits or even an opened case of beer. I should perhaps explain that beer was sold in sealed cardboard boxes of six or a dozen bottles. Alcohol could only be bought in government-controlled liquor stores and if it was given to youngsters, under the age of twenty-one and traced back to the purchaser, then the purchaser was likely to end up in court.

At a dance I once went to we were pre-warned that no alcohol was allowed on the premises. We were also told that most people would probably take bottles of Tom Collins or some other soft drink laced liberally with gin. To me, coming from the UK the liquor laws of the country seemed antiquated. Of course, it was not so many years earlier that Prohibition had been in force. An elderly cousin of mine - a little old lady when I knew her, who had lived in Moose Jaw or a similar town on the Prairies, told me how they out-witted law enforcement officers. When a raid by them was rumoured, the locals would put all their liquor into containers which they then put into the nearest lake, but not before they had attached one end of a piece of cotton to the receptacle holding the liquor and the other end to a small floating twig. Then when the police had departed the liquor would be hauled out of the lake again.

There were so many exciting places to visit. Vancouver was only a short hop by ferry or plane and Seattle wasn't much further. As well as the ski areas in the Rockies there was good skiing in Washington State, and even closer, just half an hour's drive from downtown Vancouver, at Grouse Mountain. Whistler a little further north from Vancouver hadn't been developed then, although I did hear of people being flown into the area. Of course the whole coastline was riddled with islands, and inlets gouged out by giant glaciers in the distant past. These waters not only abounded with salmon, but also attracted huge numbers of sailors. You didn't have to go off Vancouver Island to find beautiful places to visit: from the salmon fishing area of Campbell River in the North-east, to the West coast beaches, from Maple Bay where I first learnt to water ski on a rather cool evening, to the log-strewn beach of Sooke. Then there was Victoria.

Victoria was, and probably still is, a lovely, if rather quaint city. Although the provincial capital, it was dwarfed by Vancouver, its neighbour across the Straits of Georgia. The focal point of the city was the harbour and the majestic Empress Hotel. I never verified it, but I believe back in the late fifties tourists could wander into the hotel in the afternoon where they could observe dowageress types pouring tea to guests out of silver teapots. The city centre contained large numbers of tourist honey pots many with supposedly English sounding names, such as Ye Olde English Wool Shoppe! One of the principal attractions of Victoria is the famous Butchart Gardens which were created in a disused quarry, where in the summer outdoor concerts were held. A colleague on the staff used to sing occasionally at these. He had a lovely voice. A poor man's Johnny Mathis is probably a fair description of his style of singing.

One summer I took myself off in my Sunbeam Alpine for what proved to be a wonderful trip round British Columbia. I travelled up the Fraser Valley to William's Lake, having done a little detour to Barkerville on the way. Barkerville was an old gold-mining community. To reach this small settlement you had to turn off the main highway and travel some fifty miles down a dirt track. Despite its inaccessibility, it still appeared to be a successful tourist attraction. It had been renovated to look as it did back in the early 1900s with guides appropriately dressed and dummies in some of the buildings. You could even, if you wished, buy some 'pay dirt' for $1 and try to pan gold.

Much of the interior of BC is very dry, almost semi-desert. I remember one great stretch of country that had once been irrigated and farmed. It had been relatively prosperous until the men went off to war, the First World War. Many never returned and the irrigation systems fell into disrepair as there were no men to maintain the systems and eventually it reverted to an area of scrub and sage bush again.

William's Lake was then a small town in the middle of cattle ranch country. Someone once told me that a letter was sent to a resident of the town. It was addressed simply "Bill's Puddle, Canada". It apparently reached the person for whom it was intended! I was there for the rodeo. This was tremendously exciting and was also a great social occasion for the ranchers, cowmen and Indians of the area. Round the edge of the site were large numbers of tepees and trailers where the cowmen and Indians stayed for the duration of the event. In those days it had a fairly informal air about it too. All manner of cowboy skills were on show. But none were more exciting than the event where two riders would ride either side of a steer as it was released from a shute. One would jump on the back of the steer and try to wrestle it to the ground. This like the bronco riding was timed. The shute was not unlike the starting stalls at a race horse meeting. Another event which to the casual observer seemed even more dangerous was the riding of bulls. The bull, inevitably with long fearsome-looking horns with a rider already on board would come out of a shute, at great speed, the rider clinging on for dear life. Many of the riders would be ceremoniously dumped. Then they would scramble to their feet, leg it to the fence and clamber over as fast as they could. To help give them more time there was a clown in the arena with a large blown up vehicle tyre, which he used to try to distract the bull, to great cheers from the onlookers.

Canadians, especially those in more remote areas, are very hospitable. This was certainly the case in William's Lake. I had contacts there through one of the schools, but they weren't people I knew well. However I was made very welcome and came and went as I pleased. One day I decided I would take a little journey off the beaten track in my car. I had looked at a map and it appeared that there were some small dirt roads which I could take and do a round trip of say thirty or forty miles. After traveling thirty or forty miles across a landscape of grassland with patches of coniferous forest, all I had seen was a lone Indian by the river that I had crossed and numbers of cattle. I wasn't too sure where I was. To make matters worse one of the tyres punctured. This I changed watched by a few inquisitive, unfriendly-looking, cud-chewing cattle. I was also becoming rather conscious that the petrol level was beginning to drop. As luck would have it after travelling another fifteen or twenty miles I came across signs of a small logging operation where I spied a large trailer or caravan. I knocked on the door and was greeted by a filthy looking mother and child. The mother was able to inform me that there was a ranch another fifteen or twenty miles down the road. I couldn't miss it. They would be able to supply me with some petrol at the ranch. This turned out to be the case. Then I was given directions as to how to get back to a tarmac road and eventually Williams Lake. When I finally arrived back at base I found I had covered 270 miles! I subsequently learned that the ranch, where I had been able to purchase petrol was called Gang Ranch. It was one of the biggest, if not the biggest, in the world and covered something in the region of 4,000,000 acres, which I was told is about the size of Yorkshire. I subsequently learnt that a week or two earlier two English women had gone off into that area and had not been seen again!

My journey continued on to Banff National Park where I had skiied. But the area was very different in the summer. One of the attractions of visiting the National Parks of Canada is seeing the wild life. Bears, moose and other wild animals are often to be seen on the roads. There are, of course, magnificent walks in and around Banff which was a favourite place of mine. The large and imposing Canadian Pacific Hotel, a much more substantial one than the one at Shawnigan Lake, now overlooked a flowing River Bow. The landscape was no longer frozen and the golf course in front of the hotel had emerged from its winter blanket of snow. I spent one afternoon trying to track a moose with my camera. I never did get very close and only succeeded in filming a bittern. It was probably just as well as I believe Moose can have a certain antipathy towards humans and are not always the docile creatures that pictures of them might lead us to believe. Some of the walks up winding mountain tracks were delightful. The higher I got the more breath-taking the views became. All the time I was accompanied by the ubiquitous chipmunk. Occasionally I would spot a mountain goat perched precariously on a narrow mountain ledge. For those who find the walk up the mountain just too much there is often the chance of a ride down in a gondola lift. It was at the top of such a lift I discovered another North American expression that I was not familiar with. I wanted to find a toilet and seemed to have difficulty making myself understood. Eventually the person I had approached said "Oh, you want the rest room, do you?" I wasn't totally convinced as I didn't really want a rest, but I said, "Yes," and went to investigate.

While in the Banff area I made a swift visit to Calgary and took in the glaciers of the Columbia Ice-fields before returning by way of the Okanagan Valley with its countless acres of fruit trees and its own answer to the Loch Ness Monster, the Ogopogo. It was said that the Ogopogo lived in a cave at Squally Point to where the Indians would carry small animals in their canoes to appease the serpent.

The scenery in British Columbia is very spectacular. One of the most fabulous views I know is from the Malahat, on the Island Highway, where it reached its highest point. I passed this regularly on trips to Victoria. Not long before I arrived in Canada the road had been modernised and straightened. A new route had been hewn through a huge mass of rock. The actual viewpoint was a loop of the old road which clung to the cliff side. If you paused there on your journey and stood, probably five or six hundred feet up and looked east you could, on a clear day, see Mount Baker in Washington State, some 90 miles away. It looked like a giant ice cream cone. Immediately below you was a long arm of the sea. Then beyond that was the Saanich Peninsular, the most important farming area on the whole of Vancouver Island; beyond that again were the Straits of Georgia and then mainland USA and Canada.

There were other spectacular areas too. The trip to the West coast of Vancouver Island was always very exciting. To get there in those days it was necessary to travel up to Port Alberni, and then on through the forests of Douglas Firs. These huge trees, standing at over two hundred feet, were seedlings when Columbus arrived. They had to be seen to be believed. Soon after Port Alberni the tarmac road gave way to a logging track. This type of road was not very kind to private cars. To make them more level the logging companies would use a grader on them and in the summer months would spray oil to keep down the dust. But the grading often produced a sort of corrugated effect so that driving along the road was bone-shaking to say the least. There was a tendency not to volunteer your car if you intended to visit the area! If you persevered with your journey over some forty or fifty miles of dirt track you would come to the West coast of the island and a most magnificent beach some nine miles long which was, in those days, virtually deserted. Just inland from the beach a road ran parallel to it linking two small fishing communities of Tofino and Ucluelet. The Headmistress of the Strathcona, the girls' school near Cliffside, and a friend were visiting this beautiful area, now The Pacific Rim National Park, and had a minor accident that resulted in a damaged door that would not stay shut. Fortuitously the local RCMP happened to come by and, true to tradition, he lent a hand. While he was busy noting down particulars of the accident he handed the Headmistress his car keys and told her she would find some rope in the trunk (boot) of his car with which to tie up the door so they could continue their journey. Unfortunately when this was done she waved goodbye to the policeman, and set off for the little fishing village six or seven miles away at the north end of the beach. What she hadn't realised was that she had omitted to give the policeman back his car keys. As this was a very remote part of the coast and vehicles rarely came by it was two or three hours later that the poor man rather sheepishly rooted out the people he had helped. It is questionable who was more embarrassed, the Headmistress for not realising that she hadn't returned the keys or the Mountie for allowing himself to be left stranded miles from anywhere.

After four happy and exciting years I decided it was time to return to the UK. It was always going to be something of a problem finding a job back in England. It is not practical to pop back six thousand miles for a quick interview. But luck was very much on my side. Before going to Canada I used to take a cricket team over to Clifton, my old school. My opposite number at Clifton was not only a keen cricketer, but coincidentally he had studied Geography at the same college as me at Oxford, although some years earlier. It was he who suggested that when I was ready to return from Canada I could do worse than write to the Headmaster. This I did. It so happened that the person who had suggested I write to the Head was himself leaving at the end of the school year. I was offered a post which included teaching Geography and taking cricket among other things. I accepted with alacrity.

So, in the summer of 1963, I left. I was seen off from Vancouver, on the P & O ship, the Oriana, by Jim and Hilda. The journey home with stops at San Francisco, San Diego, Acapulco, the Panama Canal, Jamaica and Bermuda was exciting, but that is really another story.

Chapter 10 – Return to Clifton

One of the first things I did when I returned to England was to visit Bristol, meet the Headmaster and find out more about the job that I had been offered. It so happened that the day I arrived the Lobsters were playing cricket against one of the villages outside Bristol. The Lobsters is the name of the Clifton Preparatory School Staff Cricket Team. In those days having an enjoyable game was probably more important than winning. Two rules other than the normal Laws of Cricket as set out by the MCC applied to Lobster cricket. The first was that every one who wanted to should be allowed to bowl, and more importantly, the second was that at least one over of underhand lobs should be bowled in every match. Hence the name "Lobsters". These 'Lobs' were often bowled by the Art Master. His most telling delivery was the one that went up very high and came down almost vertically on to the top of the stumps. Because of the variety and uncertainty posed by such bowling the 'Lob' spell nearly always got wickets. Although it could not be called a rule it was understood that after the match the Lobsters would always adjourn to the nearest hostelry with their camp followers to enjoy a chat with the opposition over a pint or two.

It was strange coming back to teaching in England. As I stated earlier, in British Columbia there had been fairly rigid guide lines as to what should be taught at each level. Exactly the same books would be used at Cliffside as were use in other parts of the Province: Vancouver, Kamloops and Prince George.   This obviously hampered the ingenuity and individuality of the teacher. Back in England in 1963 such constraints hardly existed. In my earlier years at Clifton Prep or The Pre (by which name it was more familiarly known) I had a fairly free rein. This was because the majority of children moved from the Prep School to the Senior School and there were reasonable relations and good liaison between the schools. Later on it became increasingly important to prepare children for other schools than Clifton and this necessitated keeping fairly close to the Common Entrance Syllabus so that children wishing to move to schools other than Clifton would not be at a disadvantage.

I missed Canada. I missed the spectacular scenery, the Lake, the space and the friends that I had made. This I felt particularly keenly that first

Christmas after I returned. I spent it at my sister's and I well remember being really miserable because it wasn't the home I had known for the previous four years. This was no reflection on my family. It was simply that people to whom I had felt really close were thousands of miles away. It was rather like that first Christmas Eve that I spent in Banff, in reverse. Fortunately once I was back at school and I was busy this fit of blues also evaporated.

Very early on during my time back at Clifton I was asked to take up a post as Acting Housemaster of the Headmaster's House. Previously the post had assumed the name of House Tutor, but perhaps because I had been a Housemaster in Canada, or perhaps because the Headmaster, who was automatically the Housemaster, had extra burdens placed upon him as Chairman of the IAPS (Incorporated Association of Preparatory Schools), I was installed as Assistant Housemaster. To say that the Headmaster was busy is an understatement. He used to come in with lists of evenings when he would be away. One day his list covered the following 19 of the next 21 days. Fortunately, on the staff, I had good friends, who helped shoulder some of the burden.

It should be explained that the school, which then had three to four hundred pupils was big by Prep School standards. For pastoral purposes it was divided up into a number of Houses. Even the day pupils had houses where they could meet, change for games, do their prep if they wanted to do it at school, and, as it were, socialise.

The House I was to help look after was for the smaller boarders, some 30 or 40 of them aged 8 to 11. The building like most of the boarding houses, which were scattered round the suburb of Clifton in Bristol, was large and Victorian. The ceilings were high and often with beautiful moulding, but they were extremely expensive to heat. As it happened the Headmaster's wife had really run the house for the previous twenty years anyway, so things weren't likely to change that much with my arrival! Tory was in charge. There was no gainsaying that. However she was a lovely person, for whom I had great respect and affection. There was only one area with which I did not see eye to eye with her. That concerned her corgi which roamed the private side of the house. Whenever I crossed the hall which I had to do to get to my room it would come rushing up to me yapping and nipping at my heels as if I was a recalcitrant cow. After a while I learnt to peer through the door to the private side to make sure the coast was clear and, if it was, I would make a hasty rush for the stairs and hope to reach the safety of my room before it could disengage itself from whatever it was doing.

My stay as Assistant Housemaster was fairly brief, and before long I was offered a Day-boy House, North Town. It is perhaps worth digressing here to comment briefly on the Headmaster and his wife, Hank and Tory Hankey. Man and boy I served under five Headmasters at Clifton. Hank or as he was known among his 'Stage' friends Mark, was probably the most all-round of them all. This is not to denigrate the others. His immediate predecessor I hardly knew.

Subsequent Headmasters I perhaps knew better, or maybe I was in less awe of them. Certainly Hank had presence and so did his wife. I had, of course, been a pupil when he first came to Clifton. Very early on in his first term, when I was about twelve he ordained that children shouldn't hit each other over the back of the head with books - all very childish. Be that as it may, boys being boys a number took little notice. The next thing that happened was that some 15 boys were summoned to the Headmaster's study and each given two or three strokes of the cane. I mention this for various reasons. The effect was dramatic. The Headmaster had drawn clearly defined lines. We boys now realised he meant what he said. We were perhaps in awe of him, but the incident hadn't caused us to be frightened of him. From then on he rarely used the cane, but he had made his point. I don't believe this did any of the boys concerned any harm, but in one short sharp lesson we had all learned to respect our new headmaster. Sadly this couldn't have happened today. I hasten to add that I am in no way advocating a return to the bad old days where corporal punishment was widespread. However in the hands of wise and caring people it did have its uses.

I used it only occasionally when I became a Housemaster, and it was usually a gym shoe rather than a cane. Out of bed and playing around after lights out usually merited one or two wallops. The only time I remember using it in anger was with a boy who had been blatantly bullying.

The Mount (page 25)

He would also take staff for water skiing sessions (page 69)

One of the most fabulous views I know (page 74)

Julia Mary, Gill's niece, was determined to feature in at least one of the wedding photographs (page 101)

We bought a little cottage in Chew Magna (page 105)

The highlight of my sabbatical term was our World Trip (Chapter 15)

*The Canadian part of the trip was, of course,
simply an excuse to catch up with old friends*

Derek and Mary outside Shawnigan Lake School (page 131)

Jim and Hilda who were part of the original Cliffside set-up (page 131)

Sadie and Charlie gave us an enormous amount of pleasure (page 117)

The children loved to see their teachers letting their hair down

To return to the subject of my first Headmaster at the Pre - he cultivated quite a wide circle of friends outside school through music. He wrote religious music and pop hymn tunes, some of which were broadcast. He is also reputed to have played the piano occasionally in the Embassy Night Club in Leicester Square. I have that only on hearsay. Be that as it may, twice after late nights in London he returned having suffered at the hands of the criminal fraternity. On the first occasion he was allegedly coming from the Embassy and he was asked the time, at which point he was struck with a knuckle duster. On the second occasion he was walking down Regent Street when he felt something sticking in to his back and a voice demanded money. His retort was typical of him. "Don't be so silly." He was pistol-whipped and next thing he knew he was in St George's Hospital. He was much more shaken on this occasion. I remember it well because the next night he was due to take the part of the Stationmaster, who is the 'baddy', in The Ghost Train. This was the annual staff production for the children. In the true theatre tradition he insisted, "The show must go on" and took his place despite passing out at one stage and obviously being in poor shape.

These Staff Plays were always looked forward to with great excitement. The children loved to see their teachers letting their hair down and they were good entertainment when television was still in its infancy. One year, a fairly strict disciplinarian of ample proportions and nicknamed Hitler, took the part of the Good Fairy much to the delight of the children. Plays such as The Ghost Train and Agatha Christies's Ten Little Niggers were regulars. But occasionally with help from a few colleagues in the senior school we branched out and put on the Mikado or The Pirates of Penzance. These productions were very good for bonding staff and were always great fun. Sadly they don't happen any more.

Looking back over the years it seemed to me each Headmaster was appointed with a particular brief such as to increase the numbers, improve the structure of the teaching, tighten discipline, or upgrade the fabric and general appearance of the school. As I saw it the greatest strength of the in-coming Headmaster was usually the perceived weakness of his predecessor! Nowadays the Headmaster's job is very wide ranging. Teaching is perhaps the last skill that he requires, although I am still of the opinion that it is no bad thing for the Head to teach a few lessons a week just to keep in touch with what happens at the coalface. It not only keeps him mindful of what his staff face every day, but it also keeps him in contact with the children. He has not only to have an understanding of teaching, but is also expected to be an accountant, a PR expert, a diplomat, an innovator, a friend and counsellor to his staff without getting too close to them and much more besides. Some years later when I was acting Headmaster I realised how difficult it was to go, from a fairly important meeting with the School Council back to a lesson teaching twelve-year-olds. I have always felt very strongly that to get the best out of staff it is important that they know they are appreciated. This was one area at which Hank and Tory were particularly skilled. Like my first Headmaster, Hank did this by publicly expressing his thanks, and by writing little notes to individuals. Also Hank and Tory used to entertain groups of staff regularly. I look back with pleasure on the Buffet Suppers that they used to give in their lovely large dining room. In one corner was a 'Dumb Waiter', a sort of lift which was hauled up by ropes from the kitchen below. Each time it came up there was a variety of tasty dishes to be added to the array of food set before us. Hank and Tory invited selections of staff, but also invited staff from the senior school and some of their own interesting friends. The opportunity to meet people from outside the school helped to remind us that there was a world beyond Clifton.

One fairly impromptu party stands out. Sometime in the mid sixties My Fair Lady was on tour and through one of his theatrical connections Hank invited the cast to a party one night after the show. This was the start of quite a long association with those who were involved with the production. It spawned other parties as well as cricket matches between My Fair Lady cast and the Lobsters. Later, members of the cast when on tour with other productions even stayed with staff they had met on those first occasions. At least two colleagues had fairly serious relationships with members of the chorus, and in due course, the school chaplain married one of them. For me and other teachers it was an opportunity to meet and mix with stage personalities like Tony Britton, Anna Neagle, and Liz Robertson, to name a few: people whose paths in the normal run of things we would never cross.

One other skill that Hank had developed to a fine art was preaching at the Sunday Services. There was one when he walked slowly up into the pulpit, took a cigarette from his silver case, tapped it two or three times on the case, put it in his mouth, pulled out his lighter and went to light the cigarette. You could hear a pin drop. Tory, his wife, and others of us who knew him well thought that perhaps he was having a breakdown. There was a huge intake of breath. Sadly I can't remember his message, but he had captured our interest!

It was during the spell that I was attached to the Headmaster's house that an incident occurred that was a reminder that boys will be boys, and that when one is responsible for fairly large numbers of them one needs to be constantly alert. It was early evening and the matron and I were having supper by the window of her work room, which looked out on to the playground. The children of the house were playing outside prior to going to bed. Suddenly, to our amazement, a small face appeared above the roof

CLIFTON COLLEGE v MARLBOROUGH COLLEGE

on the

CLIFTON COLLEGE CLOSE, SATURDAY, NOVEMBER 14th, 1970

KICK-OFF 2.45 p.m.

Clifton v. Marlborough
20 A Side Centenary Match 1964

CLIFTON	Referee: M. H. TITCOMB G.R.F.U.	MARLBOROUGH
M. S LOCKYER	Full Back	P. K. BROOKES
B. F. W. COTTRELL		J. D. M. LEIGH
D. M. FREED	Three-Quarter	H. STORRY-DEANS
W. J. G. MULLENS	Backs	P. FARRANT
T. L. DAVIES		J. W. FIELD
H. D. EVANS	Half Backs	A. J. S. ELLWOOD
N. H. E. RIGG		D. E. GRIFFITHS-JONES
S. MIDDLETON	F	J. R. B. CROCKETT
V. H. PERRY (Capt.)	O	D. WATSON
A. W. WEAVER	R	J. M. LANDALE
D. G. G. PUDDLE	W	R. J. S. POYNTZ
D. I. HOWELL-RICHARDSON	A	J. R. WIMBLE
P. W. DAVIES	R	R. HART
A. M. SAXTON	D	C. B. DOWLING
J. T. GRIFFITHS	S	A. A. W. SYMINGTON

MATCH CARD 1/-

In aid of the Southmead Community Council
1970 CHRISTMAS PARCELS FUND FOR THE ELDERLY
Collection at half-time.

The Rugby Union Centenary Year
match proramme

The photograph shows the clifton and
Malborough Teams that replayed, a hundred
years on, the first ever match between schools

of the main school building which is all of fifty feet high. In a second the face ducked down again, but not before we had seen who it was. We rushed round to the back of the building, but the boy concerned had already reached terra firma. An even closer eye was kept on him after that.

About this time too, 1964 to be precise, the Centenary of the first ever rugby match between schools was reenacted and I was lucky enough to be invited to take part. The opposition, Marlborough, arrived at the Close, the name given to the main playing field adjacent to the school, by horse drawn coach one autumn day. There were twenty players on each side, fifteen forwards, but only five backs. All were dressed in long white trousers and distinguishing shirts. Because of the preponderance of forwards the ball rarely emerged from the melée. During the original match, apparently, the Clifton players engaged in 'hacking', which presumably would, in today's terminology, be described as 'stamping'. The Marlborough captain eventually decided that this was not very sporting and walked over to his headmaster to complain. He was told to win the game first, which apparently they did. Happily in 1964 the result was reversed, although I have to say there was only one score in it. Indeed the ball so rarely emerged from beneath the mass of forwards that it is a miracle that either team scored at all.

It is worth observing that the Close, where the Senior School played their most important cricket and rugby fixtures was the same stretch of turf of which Henry Newbolt penned the famous lines:

"There was a deathly hush on the Close tonight –

Ten to make and the match to win –

A bumping pitch and a blinding light,

An hour to play and the last man in.

And it's not for the sake of the ribboned coat,

Or the selfish hope of a season's fame,

But his Captain's hand on his shoulder smote-

Play up! play up! And play the game.

In the modern world of professional sport these words seem to have little meaning. The Corinthian spirit and the idea of playing a game to win, yes, but not to win whatever the cost, seems too often absent.

North Town, the house I moved to after I left the HM's house, catered for boys aged between 11 and 13. My stay there was brief and I can recall little of particular interest except for one small happening. It was the last day of term and we were preparing for our Christmas party. Christmas Parties were usually very noisy affairs. First a large turkey-based meal was eaten and then there were boisterous games where the children were given the opportunity to let their hair down. During the afternoon those who weren't actively engaged in the preparations were told to go off for a couple of hours and amuse themselves with the usual caveat that if they went off campus they must be accompanied by at least one other person. Just as it was getting dark one of the boys returned to say that a man in a raincoat had exposed himself to him. The Police were informed and came round and to the obvious excitement of the boy concerned he was whisked off in a police car to see if he could spot the offending person. Eventually he returned, sad to relate, without having spotted his quarry. The party started. Then more police returned to ask for more intimate details of the state of the 'flasher' and what he actually did.

Some years later there was a far more serious incident involving the police. By then Hank had retired. One Sunday morning we came over to breakfast to find a green tent on a patch of ground by the school and a number of policemen about. It transpired that a young girl had been murdered and her body found there the night before.

Hundreds of people who lived in the area were questioned. The new Headmaster of the Preparatory School had made available to the police three rooms in his house for interviewing purposes. As I remember it, the murder was supposed to have happened around 10.00pm. Answers were matched against other answers. One person is alleged to have said he was walking along one of the local roads and he saw an old lady walking her dog. This turned out be the Headmaster's wife and even her worst enemies wouldn't have called her old. It was this same dog that brought into one of the rooms where people were being questioned a contraceptive and deposited it at the feet of the person being questioned. All the staff were questioned and many of the senior boys in the Upper School. The murder had occurred on a Saturday evening and although the boys should have been in their houses a number of the older ones had crept out to the pubs and to parties. Inevitably rumour was rife and for several days it was one of the main topics of conversation in both the Upper School and the Pre.

One Housemaster of an Upper School House was asked by the police if they could question his boys. He is supposed to have huffed and puffed a bit and said there wasn't much point as they would all have been in the house. Rumour has it that very few were!

Eventually it was my turn for questioning. I was just leaving when the matron there, who obviously felt the need for spicing things up a bit, said to me in a voice sufficiently loud to be heard by the police, "Oh, Colin you know that blue duffle jacket you asked me to take to the cleaners - I've collected it for you!" It was thought that the murderer might have been wearing such a garment!

The whole incident was made more interesting by the fact that on the night of the murder one member of staff, an ex-policeman, who had a flat attached to the Headmaster's house realised that there was a lot of police activity and, perhaps rather foolishly, he decided to creep out to investigate. He was spotted and beat a hasty retreat back to his flat and then listened to descriptions of himself being broadcast on the police waveband of his radio. In fact it did him little good as he was later subjected to a considerable amount of questioning which caused him much stress.

Around the time I took over the Day-boy House I decided it was a suitable moment to invest in bricks and mortar. I eventually found a small three-storey house sandwiched between the magnificent crescents which are the heritage of Georgian Bristol. It was Number 5 Glendale and was down a steep little hill at the end of a cul-de-sac. 1, 2 and 3 had disappeared - presumably bombed during the war. Nearby were the shells of houses that had once been Hope Square, also Georgian, and now happily restored to something of their former glory. 5, 6 and 7 Glendale still stand, a little terrace of three houses. I bought Number five in 1967 for £2,000. True I spent £5,000 on it and installed central heating myself and redecorated from top to bottom. I also had one major alteration done which was to convert the top two rooms into one fairly large L-shaped room and to put in a window which had magnificent views across the roof tops to Dundry. But that same building would at today's prices fetch in the region of £300,000.

To start with, the previous owner of the house, who I knew slightly, shared the house temporarily. Then, after a while I let rooms to students. The brother of another friend who was an architectural student was my first paying guest. He and two friends moved in even before all the work on the house was finished. In fact I had almost completed the central heating and was hurrying to finish with the idea of going away for the weekend. I nailed the last floorboard down. In the rush to complete I had carelessly put a nail through a pipe. In the over-optimistic but forlorn hope that the nail was well enough wedged to prevent too much water leaking I set off. Later I phoned to check all was well. Of course it wasn't. The occupant of the room underneath the point where the errant nail had pierced the pipe spent the next 48 hours with a bucket in the middle of the room collecting the steady stream of water that came from the ceiling.

Every month or so, the architectural students had to produce projects, which involved scale models as well as much writing. Inevitably, as the date of the deadline approached, life for the students became more frenetic, and it culminated with an all night blitz. This was not because they still had much to do to complete their work. It was on account of the fact that another student, a girl, and not unattractive, who lived near by, had not actually done very much if anything towards her project. The night before the projects were due to be presented five or six of her friends would meet in her flat and between them they would put together a piece of work that could be presented in her name next day.

After the students a friend moved in. The work on the house was progressing well though still not finished. A highlight of this period was the Breakfast Party. The house had a small terrace in front of it, below which were some communal gardens, to which my father had contributed a number of shrubs. On warm Sunday mornings we used to invite friends to a leisurely breakfast. Coffee, orange juice, croissants, toast and coffee would be provided on the terrace as well as some Sunday papers. We would sit, chat and read our papers until it was time to go to our next engagement.

All this was brought to an end however when I received a request late in 1970 to take over a boarding house - Hankey's - that had only recently been opened. The previous Housemaster had tended his resignation not long after taking up residence, as he had applied for and been offered a post as a Headmaster. The Headmaster of The Pre therefore had to look hastily for a replacement. I was to move in during April the following year. The next two or three months were extremely hectic, as I had to make sure my house was in a suitable state for people to rent and at the same time prepare to move into a school boarding house.

The building that I was to move in to was a large double-fronted Victorian building with huge rooms. The 'Private Side' was made up of three sizeable bedrooms, a bathroom, a large drawing room, a study and various loos. Then in what was almost semi-basement there was the dining room, kitchen and various cold rooms, cellars and another loo. Not only did I have to furnish the Private Side, but I also had to ensure there was sufficient china, cutlery, linen and so on so that I could entertain. So with the help of my parents and the advice of a good friend, already a Housemaster, and with a small interest free loan from the school I set out to see what I could do. I had a period of frenzied activity, visiting auction rooms, stores, and the 'seconds' shop at Worcester.

As I wasn't married I had to engage the services of a Housekeeper

Also, as I wasn't married at the time, I had to engage the services of a Housekeeper. Advertisements were placed and interviews were initiated. Time was short and during term there was little to spare, so inevitably, much of the preparation for the move to the boarding house had to be undertaken during the school holidays. Early in 1971 twenty-four hours in a day seemed far too few!

Chapter 11 – Hankey's The First Five Years

The House I found myself responsible for had only opened the previous September. Before that it had been a boarding house for a local girls' school. The boys' dormitories were light and airy, but, in winter could be positively freezing. In order to try and persuade the powers that be that the heating system should be improved - it consisted of a few rather ancient storage heaters, which were sited in the recreation rooms, but there were no heaters in the dormitories - we did a survey of temperatures. During one cold snap the temperatures in the dormitories barely nudged above freezing. The 'Authorities' at the time were not impressed! However, curiously enough, I always felt that the boys in Hankey's succumbed to the normal winter ailments less than those in other houses which were properly heated. This I put down to the healthy environment!

Another perceived disadvantage that the house had - at least I'm sure it was not a good selling point to parents - was that it was five or six hundred yards to the dining rooms and other school buildings. In fact the boys never complained although they had to walk the journey to and from the House three, four, or even five times a day. I think that being a little away from the school helped to give the House a sense of identity.

Normally a Housemaster's wife was an integral part of the House 'Team', for want of a better word. She received a small allowance for her endeavours. At the time I took over the house I had no wife. The Housemaster received an allowance too and he and his family lived virtually free. Food, heating and telephone cost nothing. Other staff included a live-in matron, and a live-in House Tutor, who was really the Housemaster's assistant. Two out-house Tutors and two or three domestics and the 'House Man' completed the staff.

A word about the 'House Man' - his first job was to look after the boiler, a rather temperamental beast that needed gentle coaxing if it was to serve our needs properly. It heated the water for the whole building so when it went out, which it did from time to time, we had no hot water at all. He also had to keep the downstairs area including the changing rooms clean, put out the rubbish and do any other dirty jobs that needed doing. As well as these tasks he found time to do some tidying up outside in the garden. We had two wonderful men. The first was a Mr Lambert. He had been in the navy. He had not been an officer, but he was an extremely intelligent man. Every day he did the Times crossword and he enjoyed a hand of bridge. It was for this reason that when on board ship he often received preferential treatment. Whenever the officers were short for bridge Mr Lambert was summoned to the Officers' Mess to make up the numbers. I think he received a certain amount of ribbing for this from his colleagues, but I suspect he was well able to take care of himself. When I knew him he was already in his late sixties, and he was still an imposing man.

Because I wasn't married I required a Housekeeper to carry out some of the tasks that a wife would do, which, in nutshell was the day to day running of the domestic side of the house. Apart from ensuring the House was kept clean, over-seeing the Matron and domestic staff, her job involved washing and ironing my clothes, cooking an evening meal for the resident staff and any 'outhouse' tutor who might be on duty and occasionally entertaining.

There were between 50 to 60 boys in the House aged 11 to 13. Very roughly, half were boarders. This was a real bonus on two counts. One was because it meant that we had a relatively small number to look after at weekends. The other was that many of the parents of day pupils became good friends and, more importantly, after I married, became a way for my new wife to meet people.

Even before I was married I felt that having links with people outside school was vital. I was fortunate in that, having been at Clifton as a boy, I already knew a lot of people in the area. But I also joined the local tennis club through which I made a large number of friends, and some years later, a local golf club. The golf club was particularly important as a place I could get away from the house and school in my years as a bachelor Housemaster. I knew that once I was there on the golf course no-one could phone me up or ask me questions about any problem they might have. It was well before the days of mobile phones.

It was in these early days as a member of a local golf club that I had my 'hole-in-one'! I was on the short 17th and took a six or seven iron to the green. Unfortunately the shot was a fairly wild hook and it sailed towards the men's 18th tee which one of the groundstaff was mowing. Although I shouted, "Fore!", it was obvious he was totally oblivious to the missile that was heading towards him. I saw the groundsman wave his hand and then as we approached the 18th tee two ladies who had just left the ladies' tee – well in front of the men's – shouted out laughingly, "Holed in one!". The next thing that happened was that the groundsman put his hand into the pocket of his navy duffle jacket and pulled out a ball, which he then dropped. My ball had obviously gone full toss into his pocket. Fortunately he suffered no damage and he seemed unfazed by the incident.

As I said earlier my first headmaster had ensured he and all his staff had an afternoon off every week. He felt that this was not only an opportunity to get away from the people you were with all week, but also it was a brief opportunity to recharge batteries, to meet other people and therefore widen one's horizons. I have always felt this to be a wise philosophy. It is so easy to look no further than the school environment for social stimulation and I believe this to be narrow. By maintaining social contacts outside school one has a better perspective not only of school, but of life generally.

My first Housekeeper lasted three weeks. On paper she had seemed to fit the post perfectly. She was New Zealand born, about 26. She was a cordon bleu cook, interviewed well and wanted the job. However something wasn't quite right for her and so to my consternation, after three weeks, she departed and I was left to find a new Housekeeper. Why she wanted to leave I never discovered. Perhaps she read more in to the post than was intended and was disappointed. At all events her departure was, to say the least, inconvenient. My only experience of searching for and appointing a housekeeper had been an abject failure. Now I had to do it all over again. It had to be done immediately and during term time when there are in any case rarely enough hours in the day!

However, needs must, and in due course a new housekeeper was found and appointed. She was a middle-aged lady who had worked in a girls' boarding school in Bath. There were vibes that she was a bit bossy with children. But as she wasn't, in this case, going to be directly responsible for the children, that didn't seem really to matter. In any case there was a fairly urgent need to appoint someone and, with the one caveat already mentioned, her references were impeccable.

She wasn't perfect, but on the whole, to start with, things ran fairly smoothly. One source of trouble was her relationship with the matron which, after a honeymoon period, rapidly deteriorated, probably because she wanted to establish her authority over her. The Matron had been in residence since the inception of the House. I became the peace-maker in this small domestic spat. Eventually, I suspect, it was this problem that caused my second housekeeper to move on. She had proved a good cook and had generally looked after my welfare very well. Occasionally though she overstepped the mark. Two incidents spring to mind.

The first occurred at supper one night. We always had this meal in the dining room. On this occasion my House Tutor was dining in and also two friends of mine who were nothing to do with the school. We were just about to start when my housekeeper stood up at the end of the table and announced, "We are not going to start our meal until the person who removed Mr Millar's pants and socks from the clothes line owns up." I'm not sure who was more surprised, me or my guests.

I have mentioned Christmas parties before. They became even more boisterous in Hankey's. My philosophy was that this was the last night of term. We should give the children a really good, not to say, riotous time. Hopefully they would then do their bit by going to bed reasonably sensibly even though they were always in a high state of excitement at the thought of going home the next day. Some sixteen or so assorted adult guests were invited. Some were staff and others friends not connected with the school. They would arrive promptly at 6.30pm and be given two stiff drinks beforehand. Then each would be allotted one of the boys to act as 'host' to a sit down dinner held in the changing rooms downstairs which had been suitably cleaned up and decorated for the occasion. The guests, to some extent anaesthetized by the large gin and tonics they had just consumed, would enter into the sprit of the thing. Indeed I would go further than that and say that whereas I just about had control over the children that was not always the case with some of the adults. Eventually with the meal finished, the presents Father Christmas always delivered, were handed out. They were all named and there was one for everyone. These were carefully chosen and inevitably some of the more extrovert men found themselves with water pistols with which they inflicted enormous damage on the general decorum of the party. We then adjourned upstairs to play party games. One, which was always highly popular, involved two protagonists, usually a boy and one of the adults, blindfolded and armed with rolls of newspaper slugging it out with each other. This was a great opportunity for boys to get back at members of staff, or even vice versa. There was never any lack of boys wishing to take part! Eventually at 10.30 on the dot the party for the children ended. They went off excited but weary. Meanwhile I went to assist the matron calm the boys down and encourage them to get to bed. My guests retired to the drawing room. On one particular occasion when I returned from supervising the boys I found them involved in a mild game whereby forfeits were paid by having to remove a piece of clothing. So a small pile of discarded garments had grown in the middle of the room. Soon after my arrival my housekeeper came in. Although nothing improper had occurred, nor did it, she obviously feared the worst and although I was nearly forty years old she said in front of me and my guests, "I shall have to inform your mother about this."

A strange coincidence occurred a month or two after one of these parties. A good friend of mine, who was working for Rolls Royce, was in Karachi on business. He was staying at one of the big international hotels. One evening he was having a relaxing drink by the pool and a small boy came up to him and said, "You don't remember me do you sir?" It was the same boy who had been my friend's 'host' at one of our Christmas parties.

I suppose with such a large number of pupils from all over the globe it is not altogether surprising that such coincidences happen. I remember two or three similar situations, although curiously two of these involved people from much nearer home. One year, with a group of friends I set off for Aigua Blava, then a relatively unspoilt part of the north-eastern coast of Spain. I, at the time, drove a rather sporty little number – a Sunbeam Alpine sports car not unlike the one I had in Canada. We found a campsite just a mile or two inland and eventually retired to bed. Next morning when we woke we were amazed to find the sister and Housekeeper of one of the Senior School Housemasters in a neighbouring tent.

It was when I got home from that same trip that I had another rather rude shock. I was on duty in the playground when a small boy came bouncing up to me, all smiles and asked, "Were you, sir, last Wednesday, at 1.30pm with a young lady in a green sports waiting to cross the Spanish/French frontier." I had to admit that I was!

The other similar occurrence happened many years later in the summer before Gill and I were married. We had decided to take a holiday in Corfu. We were, one day, walking along a cliff path somewhere north of Kassiopi, when I suddenly realized that the family ahead of us were our next door neighbours (we only had neighbours on one side). The wife and mother of the family turned and greeted us warmly, and then in the same breath said, "That's wild garlic over there. It's supposed to be a good aphrodisiac!"

I suppose one of the things I learned very quickly as a Housemaster was never to be surprised at anything that happened. This is true of life, but it was especially true of running a boarding house. Another was that often it was the parents of children for whom you did very little that were most grateful. Conversely parents of children you really worked for often showed very little, if any, gratitude.

A short while before Mrs X left, her confrontations with the matron were becoming increasingly acrimonious. I had the feeling that she was getting a little restless and that if she didn't hand in her notice I might have to sack her. While this was going on I happened to go to supper with a colleague whose wife had recently had a baby. I sat next to a girl, a 'Country Cousin', employed for a short while to enable the colleague's wife to find her feet. At my friend's suggestion I floated the idea that she might be tempted to take up a more permanent post as my Housekeeper. She was tempted and when, a few days later Mrs X gave in her notice, I was not unhappy. 'Mooks' took over. She was lovely with the boys, got on with the other staff, was an excellent cook and had a lovely sense of humour, which with hindsight was one of the most needed qualities for the post.

Her cooking ability was soon tested. Not only did we have excellent meals day to day, but I had no qualms when it came to dinner parties. It was not, however, the cordon bleu qualifications of Mooks that made one particular party stand out. We had wined and dined well and had adjourned upstairs to the sitting room. Brandy and liqueurs were being circulated when suddenly a very small mouse appeared in the middle of the floor. We rubbed our eyes. Perhaps we had wined too well. But, no there was definitely a mouse in the middle of the room. As one, we swooped on it. But it was a nimble little fellow, and left us all floundering, giggling helplessly. So the chase was on. Round and round the room we all went. After a while, when it decided that it needed a breather it holed out in the sofa. There was a brief pause. Then with some encouragement from the assembled company it came out and we continued to give chase, until it was eventually cornered under the window seat. Having given us such good sport for all of fifteen or twenty minutes, we took pity on it and gently carried it outside.

Quite early on during Mooks' time as my Housekeeper it was necessary to find a cleaning lady who would come and clean the Private Side of the house. An advertisement was inserted in a local paper and Bertha duly applied and came for interview. Bertha had worked as a Housekeeper for a judge and wanted a small job for three or four mornings a week. During the discussions it was necessary for her to produce a form that displayed her age. She was very worried. "You won't tell Mr Millar, will you?" she asked. For she feared if I knew that she was 76 I would not appoint her! However she was appointed and she stayed with me till she was well into her 80's. One of her little idiosyncrasies was that if she was around she always liked to answer the front door bell. Even if I was standing right beside her, she would shuffle off and open the door. On being asked if I was in, she would say, "I'll go and see", leave the person on the door step and come and find me and ask if I wanted to see the individual. Another characteristic was that she loved her food. I can still see her tucking in to a very large plate full at our wedding four or five years later.

The colleague and friend who suggested I should sound out Mooks as a possible Housekeeper was a source of strength and encouragement in those early days as a boarding Housemaster. He helped me enormously in the setting up of the House in the first place, and was always there to lean on when there were problems. This was especially important as I was still not married. There was a world of difference between looking after day boys as I had in North Town, albeit till perhaps as late as 7.30pm, and looking after boarders for twenty-four hours. I remember in the 1981 Census the question came up: "How many hours do you work?" Answer: "24 hours a day." Rightly or wrongly I felt that the most important part of my work was not in the classroom, but the pastoral care of the children in the house. This perhaps understandably wasn't always the view of house tutors. Although I tried to treat day pupils and boarders alike, when it came to the crunch, day pupils were only a phone call away from their parents, whereas for boarders we were in loco parentis. In some cases their parents lived on the other side of the globe.

Inevitably a good housemaster and his staff get to know their children very well. In those days the house staff always shared an evening meal together. This was cooked by my housekeeper and served in the dining room. One of the main advantages of this was that it was an opportunity to discuss children, mention problems and generally pool our knowledge. That is not to say we did nothing but talk about the children. But I remain convinced it contributed towards good pastoral care.

Pastoral care was what I had in mind when I went to visit one of the boys in a local private hospital. It was a beautiful warm summer's day. The boy in question had had his tonsils and adenoids removed. Although his parents were English they were at the time working in Nigeria, I believe, and I thought the least I could do was to go and see how he was getting on. However I don't cope very well with blood and hospitals. I walked into the room he was in and became distinctly clammy, so I retreated to the nurses' room. I didn't need to speak. The nurse on duty took one look at me and proffered a chair. When I felt I could get out of the hospital without collapsing in a heap I rushed back into the ward and told the startled lad that I understood he was making good progress and hastened out of the hospital as fast as my wobbly legs would take me. That was not, however, the end of the story. After Chapel the following Sunday a parent shouted over to me, "Colin, I hear you were nearly a patient at St Mary's the other day!" She was, apparently, a physiotherapist at the same hospital and the news had spread!

Round about this time we also had a Nigerian boy in the house. I marvel now at how he coped. He was a Muslim and one of a large number of children of a successful Nigerian businessman. I understood his mother was the sixth and favourite wife. He was expected to attend Chapel and generally conform. He was a cheerful individual and a fine athlete. He not only coped remarkably well given his very different cultural background, but he also had a nice sense of humour. The boys in the house were at that time only allowed a few pounds pocket money a term. This was handed in to the House Tutor for safe-keeping. It also helped to ensure that all the boys had roughly the same amount of money to spend. The boys could then draw out small sums from him when they needed it. One day, not long before the Nigerian boy left us, I happened to be with him at a railway station waiting to see him safely on to a train, when he took out his wallet and allowed me to see, probably on purpose, his Halifax cash card. When he realized I had seen it his face broke into a huge grin. He had obviously never been short of cash!

Many of the parents became good friends. Most were extremely supportive, but inevitably there were those that one didn't see eye to eye with. Occasionally, dare I say it, I felt perhaps we understood the child better than the parents. I remember we had a case of shop-lifting from a local store. Those involved were perhaps the last we would have suspected. I talked it through with the boys, letters of apology were sent to the proprietor of the shop and the boys had to make good what they had stolen. But we didn't inform the parents. I felt that the father of one of the boys, once he had been convinced that his son really had been involved, would have taken action that would have been so drastic that it might well have spoiled his relationship with his son for ever. It was a hard decision, but it seemed at the time, given the circumstances, the right one. I am as certain as I can be that that particular child did not transgress in that way again.

Another incident occurred around this time which is worth relating. Although I did what I thought was right then, I sometimes wonder, with hindsight, if there wasn't a better solution. I had received a phone call from a mother who wanted to come and see me. She seemed a very normal person and, at a recent drinks party I had given for parents, she had been one of those people who seem instinctively to know how to be helpful, passing food around and generally making sure that people were at ease. I proposed that she should come to the House or that I should visit her in her home. Both suggestions were turned down. She then suggested meeting in a small car park near by at 8.00 pm. Alarm bells began to ring, but I agreed. Just before the appointed time I told my Housekeeper and House Tutor where I was going and asked them to note the time. When I arrived at the appointed place I found that there was no lighting. Peering through the gloom I spied the side lights of a car at the back of the park. Leaving my car in the road, and taking my courage in both hands, I wandered up to the car. I looked inside and then seeing it was indeed the lady I was expecting to meet I clambered in and asked her what the problem was. "I can't get you out of my mind" was the reply. I mumbled something about not knowing what I could do about that and fled! I reported back to the House and asked that the time of return be noted. In due course I informed the Headmaster of what had happened.

Next day I received a somewhat vitriolic letter to the effect that I should have shown some sympathy and understanding. All she wanted was a shoulder to lean on. Her brother was dying and her husband did not understand her. Apparently a policeman who had come by later had been suitably sympathetic.

One of the perks of living in a school boarding house at this time was a fairly generous entertainment allowance. We had parties usually once a year for parents to enable them to meet other parents. Senior boys used to pour out drinks and hand around nibbles. It was indirectly the result of this that a minor crisis developed. The boys did such a good job that I was asked if I would let them do the same for a colleague, who wished to give a farewell party. The party was held on a grassy area by the main school buildings following the normal Sunday morning Chapel Service. It was a glorious sunny day and the guests were offered a cider cup. The boys did their bit very well, but it was thirsty work and eventually one of the boys asked the host if they might have a drink. "One," they were told. There were in fact no soft drinks available. Unfortunately they tasted it and it seemed so innocuous that one became two, then three and probably as many as six.

None of the adults had observed this. Having completed their task they headed for lunch. It was during lunch that those on duty realised something was not quite right. The boys who had been helping at the party were becoming noisy and slightly obstreperous. They were undoubtedly drunk! So they were taken back to the House and up to one of the dormitories. When we reached the dormitory we found one was missing, so a search party was sent out and this small boy was discovered weaving his way along the pavement that happened to pass the main entrance to Bristol Zoo. "Are you all right?" he was asked. His speech, somewhat slurred, he replied, "Yes, I'm just trying to find my way home."

'The Hankey's Drunks' as the other boys dubbed them were safely gathered in. Advice was sought from the staff at the school sanatorium. "Black coffee and a good sleep," was the prescribed remedy. They were left to sleep it off though initially one of the staff stayed with them to ensure there were no complications. At 5.30 pm Enoch, one of the more lively boys in the House, decided he needed to see how they were - he probably went upstairs on the pretext of wanting to collect something from his dormitory . He brought back the message that the 'Hankey's Drunks' had had enough of being incarcerated and wanted to join in with the other boys who were going for a swim. There was no sign of the hangover that they undoubtedly deserved!

I mention Enoch because he was involved in another incident that sounds fairly alarming, but wasn't quite as bad as might appear. It was a Sunday afternoon and the boys had been told to go off and amuse themselves, with the usual warning that they must sign out in the book where they were going and who they were with. Under no circumstances were they to be on their own. I hasten to add that in today's climate, I am pretty certain that I would not have allowed 12 to 13 year old boys out on their own. Having said that, I believe that this is very sad. Children have a sense of self-preservation, and they need to test themselves in the real world.

To return to that particular Sunday afternoon - most of the boys had dispersed and things were fairly quiet when one of them returned and announced casually that Enoch was clambering up and down the side of the Clifton Gorge. I had visions of him clinging on to cliff ledges with a drop of two hundred feet below. I knew roughly where he would be found, so leaving the matron to hold the fort I hastened to the spot. In fact where he and his friend were it wasn't precipitous and they weren't in any great danger, but for my peace of mind they were persuaded to return to the house.

It is perhaps worth observing that ensuring the boys had plenty to do in their spare time was important. Inevitably the more sporty children were more easily amused, especially if the weather was reasonable, as they could always go round the corner to the nearest playing field and kick a ball about or play cricket. Numerous indoor games were provided as well as two snooker tables - one half-size and one quarter size - and a table tennis table. Each term billiard, snooker and table tennis competitions were organized for which there were prizes at the end of term. There was a piano, television set and computers. Various school clubs provided opportunities for the boys to paint, model, do woodwork, and act and so on. One feature of our house was the Rag Room. This was copied from my first school. It was a bare room, where the boys could kick a football and generally let off steam without doing any damage. In an effort to keep the boys busy at the end of term we devised a magazine competition. The clearing teams each had to produce a magazine of comment on the term. As with other competitions a prize was awarded for the best.

The weekends could drag a bit. Saturday was not unlike any other day. There were lessons in the morning and then there were normal games and matches in the afternoon. On Saturday evening in the winter we provided a suitable video for them to watch before going to bed.

On Sunday we often had to go to Chapel, after which the boys were free. Frequently parents would visit and take their offspring out. Dayboys too invited their boarding chums for the rest of the day. So there were usually only a handful left and it wasn't difficult to help them to amuse themselves.

On the rare Sundays, like the first Sunday of term, when there were a large number of children not going out we usually tried to organize something such as a treasure hunt or a photo quiz. The latter involved the children being split into small teams and being given sheets of photos taken in the Clifton area. They had to find and identify the buildings shown in the photos or answer questions based on them.

Being a bachelor housemaster is a lonely job. However good the supporting staff are, and, for the previous 3 or 4 years, I had been very lucky in this respect, there is never really anyone to share problems with. Perhaps, I thought, I could revert to being a Day Housemaster. I began to drop hints about the way I was thinking. Then Gill, or 'Sweetie' as she has always been to me, came into my life, almost by accident. A mutual friend who had shared a flat in London was lodging with me during the summer holidays. She had a temporary job in Bristol and having just decided to get married she wanted a party to celebrate. She spoke to Gill and invited her for the weekend. Gill was told there was plenty of room. "A middle-aged 'batch' runs this school boarding house, but he'll be doing his own thing and you probably won't see him," she said over the phone. My wife-to-be arrived, travel-worn but as pretty as a picture and travelling light for the only time in her life. I offered her a restorative gin and tonic. That was the start of a very happy weekend. The middle-aged 'batch' was around for the whole of it. It was also the beginning of a new phase in my life.

Chapter 12 – Hankey's Married at Last

3rd April 1976 was a cold, blustery day, but the excitement of the occasion kept us warm. What a day to remember! We had decided to have the wedding in the School Chapel and the reception in Big School, which is the Senior School dining room and situated on the other side of the quadrangle from the Chapel. Gill's father had died when she was only sixteen and although Gill's mother pulled out all the stops to make it a happy day for us, we wanted to be able to support her as much as possible and it would have been difficult if the wedding had been on the Wirral. But the main reason we wanted the wedding in Bristol was that the School Chapel is such a lovely building and was very much a part of our lives. It was in reality our local church. At the time we were married it had seldom been used for weddings as a special license was required. Ours was not to be a big wedding, but we intended follow it up with a party for friends whom we couldn't invite to the wedding, when we returned from our honeymoon. Gill's Mother and other members of her family stayed in a hotel on the edge of the Avon Gorge. This has a magnificent setting with spectacular views of the gorge itself and the Clifton Suspension Bridge. My parents stayed in Hankey's. Unlike today when weddings sometimes start early afternoon and don't finish till midnight, ours was short and very sweet. One minute I was waiting nervously on the steps of the Chapel for my bride to arrive, and the next we were being whisked away by our best man in his car to where we had hidden ours in order to prevent it being sabotaged. With hindsight perhaps the wedding celebrations were all a bit too quick! But we savoured every moment: the actual service in the Chapel complete with a choir of boys from Hankey's, who among other things sang Love Divine All Loves Excelling as we signed the Register; the stirring organ music including Vidor's Toccata played by a friend and colleague; the photograph session on the steps of the Chapel, with young Julia Mary, Gill's niece, aged six, who had wanted desperately to be a bridesmaid, making sure she featured in at least one of the photographs; and the reception, with speeches from Herbert, a friend of the family, and Andrew, my Best Man. As we departed waving to our friends, Andrew suggested we go through the Memorial Arch out of the school campus, round the block and back, so we could wave again to our friends. Thank goodness no-one got mown down as we hurtled round!

Gill took to being a Housemaster's wife like a duck to water. Occasionally, during the holidays, she would head off north to see her Mother, who still lived on the Wirral. The first time she did this I decided to surprise her by putting up some decorations in the bedroom to welcome her back. I went to work and strung up across the bedroom little flags with letters on them. Unfortunately I hadn't noticed that I had misspelt the last word. The bunting read - "WELCOME HOME SWETTIE" It wasn't the most tactful welcome!

I always wished that I had kept a note of all the howlers that I came across in children's work. There are the obvious ones like the "He raped the parcel"' and one attributed to a teacher in a report "Spelling week." But the only unusual one that I have remembered and it still makes me chuckle is the description of Long John Silver. "He was a man with one leg and a bird on his crutch."

Good staff were essential for a well run House. We were generally lucky. Our House Tutor at the time I married was delightful, and although he took his teaching seriously, he had the welfare of the children in the house very much at heart. Matrons were usually young girls, who wanted a short term job. The three qualities that they most needed, apart from a sense of humour were a level head, adaptability, and a good rapport with boys of the 11 - 13 age group. They also needed the ability to get on with other people and sense of responsibility. If Gill was out they were only a phone call away from medical help at the school sanatorium. Indeed good common sense was a prerequisite of House Tutors as well. One resident house tutor was taken ill in the middle of a term and we called on the help of an eighteen-year-old who was waiting to go into the navy. Despite his youth and lack of experience he was as good as any tutor that I worked with.

It was important that all staff could be trusted and that they were always conscious that they were role models. Inevitably we were let down from time to time. However I am glad to say this happened very rarely. One occasion was during the World Cup. The boys were soccer mad and wanted to stay up late to watch a match on Television. But we had told the staff that it was too late and bed times were to be as normal. We had gone out, but for some reason we returned around 10.30 pm, earlier than expected, and found a number of the boys in the Matron's sitting room watching the match. This was not an isolated incident, but the final straw and the Matron was told she would have to go. In fact she was off at crack of dawn next day, waved off sorrowfully by her loyal fan club. Gill and I, of course, were looked upon as ogres and, for twenty-four hours at least, the boys had great difficulty in talking to us at all! But very quickly all was forgotten, a new matron was installed and things got back to normal with one exception, and this seemed to be linked. We started to receive a number of unpleasant phone calls late at night. The calls were traced back to a pay phone in a local factory where we suspect our Matron's boyfriend worked 'nights'. We took steps to put a stop to these. After a little while they ceased and peace reigned again.

That is, of course, not strictly true. Peace never really reigned in a school boarding house. One never knew what was round the corner.

As I mentioned earlier the building was large Victorian building. At one time there was a bus stop opposite the boys' entrance. It was sited there primarily for zoo visitors. Tacked on the back of Hankey's was a slightly run-down conservatory, where children used sometimes to practice their musical instruments. On one occasion one of the boys was practicing his trumpet. Admittedly he wasn't very good and it was a little hard on those with sensitive hearing. But we were amazed when someone, who had been queuing at the bus stop opposite, marched in and told the boy to stop!

Coming from the street the first room that you come to is the TV room. This was a large room with a few rather decrepit sofas and lots of bean bags. Sofas seemed to have an extremely short life span when used by 11 to 13 year old boys. One early evening a couple of the boys rushed up to me all of a twitter. "Sir! Sir!" they said, "Two people have just come in and they went into the TV room and they've turned on the Television." I don't know if they were more concerned that the television had been turned on before the permitted hour, or that they objected to people they didn't know walking in unannounced. At any rate I asked the intruders politely to leave. Fortunately they did without fuss. Soon after that we became the first House in the school to install combination type locks on the boys' entrance door.

It was in this same room that we heard a noise behind the blocked off fireplace. It didn't take a great deal of intelligence to work out that it must be a bird of some sort. We called in one of the school maintenance staff, who removed the sheet of board that had been used to seal up the old fire place and there in the grate was a huge young and very indignant seagull, which showed little gratitude for being rescued. Just the opposite - it flapped its wings vigorously and pecked at its rescuer with its vicious looking beak.

The heating was supplied by storage heaters and the building as a whole was reasonably warm. However the boys' dormitories, as I have already indicated, could be positively freezing. Periods of Arctic weather brought its problems apart from the inconvenience of waste pipes of the basins in the dormitories freezing up. I'm not sure that all the boys were as worried about this as I was because it meant that frequent washing was not very practical! But far more serious problems resulted from one particular cold snap. One morning not long after the inevitable thaw had set in the fire alarm went off. It was during the holidays and there was no hint of fire on the private side of the house. So we cautiously crept through to the other side only to discover that water, pouring from the roof space through three floors to the changing rooms, had set off the alarm. It transpired that a pipe attached to one of the tanks in the roof had been cracked and the water had probably been pouring down for some time before it set off the alarm. The mess was appalling, and although we could call upon help to clear up it was all very depressing.

We had a soaking on our side of the house too and I suspect that this could have been a contributory factor to the Dry Rot that afflicted the building. As anyone who has had the misfortune to have had an attack of Dry rot it is an insidious fungus that consumes wood. Given the ideal conditions of warmth and moisture it can travel at up to 4 metres a year.

We first discovered we had it when the ceiling of one of the lavatories on the ground floor collapsed. Fortunately no-one was enthrowned at the time. The fungus was traced from there upwards and found to be in the wall of our magnificent staircase. The reason it had got into the wall and travelled along it was that the wall was constructed only one brick wide. However in order to give it added stability a length of wood 2inches by 4, or similar proportions, was inserted along its length. The fungus stretched its tentacles along most of this length of wall. Consequently much of the wall had to be rebuilt.

The building had been fully refurbished just before I moved in so not a great deal was done during the first few years. Later on it was decided that the woodwork on the outside of the building should be renovated. This involved scaffolding all round the house and proved something of a nightmare as inevitably scaffolding is a temptation to small boys. Sure enough one afternoon I was standing outside on the pavement talking to a parent when out of the corner of my eye I spotted a movement. I looked up to see a small face peering down from the top level. The face darted back, but not quite quickly enough!

We were very fortunate in that the house had a more or less self-contained apartment or 'Private Side' and also a fairly large garden, both front and back. I derived enormous pleasure from gardening. Mowing the lawns I found particularly therapeutic. The back part which was accessed through the kitchen door and the patio that I had created not long before our wedding, was pleasantly secluded. However the building at the bottom end of the garden which housed the Senior School Mathematics and IT departments, was enlarged and modernized. Windows were put in on the second floor overlooking not only our garden, but our neighbours' as well. My plea to have these windows glazed with frosted glass was at last heeded. But of course it didn't prevent adolescents, when staff were out of the room, from leaning out of the opened windows and shouting obscenities at our dogs and bombarding them with paper darts! I found this unattractive behaviour hard to stomach. So one quiet Sunday, I fetched a ladder, and climbed up to the windows. I was armed with a drill and it was only a few minutes work to drill holes through the windows into the frames. Screws were inserted and the job was finished off with some putty and a coating of white paint. It gave me great pleasure after that to watch shadowy figures, behind the frosted glass, attempt, without success, to open the windows. So peace was restored to our garden!

Quite early on in our marriage we sold our house in Clifton and bought a little cottage a few miles out in the country, at a place called Chew Magna. It was next door to a pub, the Queen's Arms, and only a few yards from the river Chew. The Chew meandered its way harmlessly through the village. Normally it was only a few inches deep and we had been assured that although it had caused flooding in the past, work had been done to prevent this happening again. We used to go out to our cottage on our Thursday afternoons off and sometimes at weekends when we were not on duty. Occasionally we would take food and wine so that we could entertain. It was lovely place to relax and have a few hours away from Hankey's. The worst part was packing up to go home. If we had had guests we had to clear up after everyone else had left and then eventually head back to Bristol in the early hours of the morning. Despite the assurances we had had that flooding was a thing of the past, one night, after a period of snow followed by heavy rain, we received a phone call from the Bath police at around one o'clock in the morning to say that there was a Flood Alert and we should go and check that the cottage was all right. So after waking our House Tutor, so we could tell him we had to leave him in charge, we drove bleary-eyed to Chew Magna. The mild stream, that normally posed no threat, was now a raging torrent and was already over-flowing its course. We hastily moved as much furniture as we could upstairs and piled other pieces on tables. We had just about done what we could when the muddy waters at last began to pour in through the front door.

I suppose you could say some good came out of this seemingly dreadful event. When we had bought the cottage Gill had insisted that we have a lovely bright blue carpet. As soon as it was laid we knew we had made a mistake. So when the waters subsided - they seemed to disappear through the floor - and we were left with a hitherto brilliant blue carpet covered in brown slime we were able, courtesy of our insurers, to purchase a new carpet. This time we chose, appropriately, a sludgy green colour.

A year or two later the waters engulfed our lovely cottage a second time after a period of heavy rain. Much the same happened. There was the call from the police in the middle of the night, the frantic dash to move as much as we could upstairs and then the wait for the waters to subside. The only difference was that this time the local fire department appeared on the scene to give us some moral support and to pump the water out for us. However most of the water once again disappeared through the floor.

A corollary of this was that some years later when we tried to sell the house a local busy body, so we were informed, used to appear, whenever prospective buyers came to visit the house. He would apparently make himself known to them and then give them graphic details of how, when the river overflowed its banks, it would surge through the house. When we heard this we began to wonder if we would ever sell the place. Fortunately the Landlord of the Queen's Arms, next door, became wise to this and discouraged the practice!

Among the responsibilities of the wife of a Housemaster was a certain amount of entertaining.

When entertaining, there is often the problem of hinting to the guests when it was time to go. I remember many years earlier, when I was a boy and my mother was away, my father and I were invited to supper. Our hosts were an ex-Housemaster of Harrow and his wife who were friends of my parents. They had obviously over many years invited numerous boys to supper and had got the routine to a fine art. After supper we sat down and chatted. The Housemaster's wife was in good form. She knitted away furiously and whenever conversation flagged she fired questions at us as one to the manner born. But at 10.30 pm on the dot she wrapped up her knitting and stopped asking questions – it was clearly time for Father and me to go!

There was also for Gill the day to day feeding of the resident staff and any outside staff who might be on duty. Even on our Thursday afternoons off Gill would always leave a prepared meal for any staff, who had to stay in.

Our biggest social event was the annual Sports Day or Commemoration as it was more often called. The day included a Chapel service, exhibitions, athletics events and lunch in the Houses. So it was usual for us to entertain approximately a hundred and twenty parents and others to lunch. The days leading to this event, without doubt, for children and staff, were frenetic. It had become something of a tradition that we should do the catering ourselves. Salmon from a local fishmonger's had been ordered weeks ahead. This was duly delivered. Strawberries were collected the previous day from a farmer near Cheddar. Then on the Friday itself it was all hands to the pump. Extra hands were drafted in including both our Mums. At around 5.30 am Gill and I would set off to the local wholesale fruit and vegetable market, a veritable Aladdin's Cave. Not only were we able to purchase the salad needed, but also flowers, and plants for the garden as well. Once back at Hankey's we switched into top gear. The cleaners had already arrived and were busy polishing the place. Most of the furniture moving had been done by the boys the night before. A gang of youthful volunteers was employed to hull the strawberries - always a popular task as inevitably some of the strawberries found their way down the throats of those doing the hulling. All available help was summoned to the kitchen to help prepare the food. Time was precious, as Gill and I had to go to the Chapel Service at 10.45am. The boys too had to be gathered in, and scrubbed and checked before they too were released to Chapel. The Service was always a highlight of the school year. Everything was carefully rehearsed in the weeks before. The choir had been fine-tuned by the choir master and even the children in the congregation had been put through their paces. The sermon was always given by a bishop or some other worthy. After the service children and parents were herded in to the marquee for speeches. This was a fairly complex operation. The idea was to keep the parents and children separated in order that the speeches could start promptly. Remember that many of the children hadn't seen their parents for weeks or even months and if they mingled at this precise point it would take considerably longer to get them all in their seats. So the parents were guided out of the main entrance into one end of the marquee and the children were directed out of another exit to the other end of the marquee. I suppose for the children the period of speeches was a rather boring interlude before lunch, which was followed by the athletic sports. For the parents it was an opportunity to hear the Headmaster and Chairman of Council speak about the school's successes and the way forward. There was usually a reminder that GCE and A Level League Tables weren't everything and that the wise parent should look at the facilities, and more importantly, the pastoral care provided by the school. In any case Exam results are, to a considerable extent, determined by intake and Clifton has always opened its doors fairly wide, particularly during the last thirty or forty years. I have strong views that education is about much, much more than simply enabling children to pass exams, important though that is. Clifton has had a relatively liberal tradition and for that reason has, I believe, prepared children for life far better than many schools that have more impressive GCSE and A Level results.

Probably the school's biggest sporting rival was the Dragon School. We were in those days of a similar size and large numbers of teams from the two schools met up once a year to do battle on the rugby field. There was a sense of occasion about these meetings. Whenever we went to Oxford we were always royally entertained. I remember, one year when our 1st XV was particularly weak I said to a colleague, "Never mind, by the time you have finished lunch you won't care who wins!"

For a number of years we, in Hankey's, acted as hosts to Staff and parents accompanying the teams to Clifton. We endeavoured to match the hospitality given to us in Oxford. One particular year Dave Allen, the comedian, was among the camp followers. I can see him now. He was standing by the door leading through to the boys' side of the house. Two boys had come to the front door as their door was locked while they were out at lunch. As they passed him, he gave them each a piece of bread and said in a quiet voice and without any expression at all, "Bless you my child."

Another highlight in the calendar, from the boys' point of view, was Guy Fawkes Night. We would gather in the back garden at the appointed hour and the display would begin. At one time we had a parent of two of the boys in the House who was involved with a munitions factory and he used to supply us with a small number of 'thunderflashes' which went off with a colossal bang, causing the whole area to shudder with each detonation. After the fireworks we all crammed into the kitchen where hot dogs and drinks were doled out. We had one or two Jewish boys in the House and questions were inevitably asked about the sausages. "Are they pork?"

"No. You can eat them," was always the supply!

It all became more complicated when we had an Indian boy in the House as well! But in the melée I don't think anyone really minded. As the saying goes, "What the eye doesn't see the heart doesn't bleed over." It always amused me, though, that some of the Jewish boys conveniently forgot their religious scruples when a plate of crispy bacon was presented to them at breakfast.

Chapter 13 Parents, Boys, Girls and Small Animals

It has to be said that Gill's training for life as a Housemaster's wife left something to be desired. She had had a spell as an air hostess, worked in a bank notably as the chief cashier in the bank that handled Harrods' takings and then up to the time she walked into my life she had been an Assistant Buyer for The Scotch House. Nor had she taken cooking very seriously up to this point. Entertaining was largely a question of purchasing an extra large portion of Chicken Chow Mein from the local Chinese Takeaway. Add to this the fact that she had no brothers it is clear to see that she was ill-prepared for her new life as wife of the Housemaster of a boys' boarding house. However daunted she may have been by the prospect it was certainly not apparent.

She soon proved to have a wonderful rapport with the children. Although I was a teacher I always felt our first priority was the welfare of the children.

Most of the parents were very cooperative, and many were appreciative of our efforts to care for their offspring and make them happy. But it is a curious fact that often it was the parents whose sons were most well-rounded and least trouble that showed most appreciation, while the parents of those that we spent hours trying to help showed little if any appreciation at all. Perhaps that tells us something!

One particular child, shall we call him Michael, had been poorly for some days. Earlier in the week we had sent him to see the doctor and he had been kept in bed in the house for a day or two. Eventually on the last day of term, we let him get up and he went off to breakfast. I spotted him when he returned, sitting down in an armchair looking very grey. I asked him if he was all right. He assured me he was. But then, it was the final day of term, the day of the Christmas Party and the last thing he wanted was to miss that! Despite his assurances I sent him to Gill who in turn sent him to the San to see the Doctor again. It was decided by the Doctor that he should be kept there under the observation of trained nurses. Although all the House staff, including Gill, were working flat out to prepare for the party, Gill still found time to take a small bag of goodies up to Michael, who was now in bed in the Sanatorium, which was about 300 or 400 hundred yards away. He was going to miss the party, but Gill didn't want him to miss out completely. At

6.30 pm, just as the adult guests were arriving, I received a phone call from the San to say that Michael was diagnosed as having appendicitis and would I take him immediately to a small private hospital nearby. Having carried out this errand, I returned to the party, but before joining the guests I had to try to contact Michael's parents in Germany. This proved to be impossible. Eventually I managed to speak to Michael's grandmother, who lived in South Wales. At 9.30 pm, with the party now in full swing I phoned the hospital to find out how the operation had gone, and was told that it had gone well, but that Michael was, in fact, suffering from peritonitis. However he was responding well. This information was relayed to Granny, and, of course, to the other boys, who were obviously concerned. Despite the timing of this incident, I felt we had done all and more than we could have been expected to do. However Michael's father, apparently, phoned the Headmaster to query our handling of the situation. Some parents seemed to take little interest in their children except when things went wrong!

Mention of the San, puts me in mind of a rare racial incident. The Matron was rather distressed to discover that one of her patients who shared a room with Wayne, a huge boy of West Indian extraction, had been beaten up. The Matron tried to get to the bottom of the problem. She questioned the boy who had been on the receiving end. He told her that he had done nothing except offer Wayne some fruit. In due course Wayne was confronted by his housemaster who knew him to be something of a gentle giant. Eventually the truth emerged. "Well Sir," he said, "After Tommo said to me, for the third time, 'Have a banana, you great ape,' I blew my top!"

Michael's illness was one crisis that stands out. Inevitably there were others. Another that remains vivid in our memories again occurred at the end of a term. End of term is, of course, a time when everyone is tired and the children are excited. It was probably a Sunday late in March. The children were amusing themselves. Many of them were tidying up and throwing away rubbish. A small group had gone to the school theatre to help clear up there after the School's Christmas Production. I was working in my study, which overlooked the garden and yard. Suddenly the relative calm was broken by one of the boys rushing into my study screaming at the top of his voice. He was obviously badly burnt - mainly his face and hands. We rushed him to the children's hospital and then from there to the Burns Unit at Frenchay Hospital, where he eventually made a full recovery. In due course he informed us that he had been by the incinerator, a brick built construction that was at the far end of the yard, and that something among the rubbish had exploded. Initially we took his explanation at face value and we were very worried. We wondered if perhaps we should have foreseen such an accident happening. But eventually the truth came out. One of the other boys sensibly came and told us. It transpired that the boy had been helping to clear the stage set after the final performance at the theatre. He had come across a firework that should have been ignited by some sort of electronic device. It had failed to go off. He, like many small boys, was curious, and although those who were clearing up had been told expressly that on no account were they to remove any unexploded fireworks, he took one off and with a match tried to ignite it. It blew up in his face with frightening consequences.

Another memory of a rather bizarre kind happened when I was taking a small group of boys for golf. It wasn't, perhaps a crisis, but it was certainly very unpleasant. We had set up a mini golf course. After a short lesson the boys were given instructions that they should never walk behind any one who was swinging a club and they were also told that if they were playing a shot they should make sure that there was no-one behind them. Then they were dispatched in pairs to distant parts of the field so that each pair could play a different hole. All went well for a while and then I saw one of the boys crawling around on the ground. It transpired that this particular boy had failed to observe the precautions I had urged upon them. A club had hit him in the mouth and knocked some of his teeth out He was scrabbling around looking for them. I do remember he was very brave, but it was a salutary lesson.

In those days, it was, by the very nature of things, more difficult to communicate with parents, who lived abroad. This was before the age of e-mails and faxes. Most of those who lived abroad were very supportive. I have always maintained that being away from parents for longish periods does not rule out loving relationships between children and their parents. But like any relationship it requires hard work and, at that time, the weekly letter was probably the vital link in this relationship. I remember how much I looked forward to the letter I received each week from my mother. Indeed I continued to receive this weekly letter from her even when I moved to Canada during my mid-twenties. For many of the boys in Hankey's that weekly letter was just as important. When the post arrived in the morning those who received regular letters from home couldn't wait to collect and open them.

This difficulty in communication is well illustrated in one particular case. I had been frustrated in my efforts to contact a parent whose son was about to start in Hankey's the following term. She had recently remarried and was living in Africa. Eventually this small boy simply arrived on our doorstep. Although he was only eleven, he had travelled all the way from Harare on his own. When he reached Heathrow, he caught a train and eventually late in the afternoon reached Hankey's looking amazingly relaxed. Some weeks later we eventually made contact with his mother and step-father!

It is perhaps worth observing at this point that I was opposed to allowing the boys to use the phone. This may sound unfeeling, but a long distance phone call could be very unsettling to a child especially one who had just started boarding. Most children are adaptable and settle into boarding life very quickly, particularly if there is plenty for them to do. Having said that I do believe that it is, on the whole, easier for a child to adapt to boarding at the age of eight than at the age of eleven. Inevitably the most likely time for a child to want to phone home is when he is feeling a bit low. Phoning home, to my mind, not only exacerbates the problem as far as the child is concerned, but it can also be very distressing for the parents and particularly Mums. After an emotional phone call from a child claiming to be unhappy it is sometimes hard to convince parents that their son, not ten minutes earlier, had appeared as happy as a sandboy, and that the reason he was feeling low was that he had probably just had an argument with one of his chums. Most parents accepted our guidance on this matter, but there were always some who insisted on speaking to their children on the phone, just occasionally of course, with good reason. Another problem with in-coming calls was that as the children led fairly active lives it wasn't always easy to locate them.

On one occasion a father phoned and was left waiting while I went in search. Something distracted me while I was looking for the boy concerned, and when I returned to my study some twenty minutes later I was horrified to discover the phone still off the hook. I picked it up again, informed the father that his son was just coming, and went off in search again. Perhaps the parent got the message as I don't remember that particular parent phoning up to ask to speak to his son too often after that!

As I put the finishing touches to this it is now 2003. I believe anyone in the Senior School can have a mobile, but, I was told, "They are expected to have them turned off during lessons!" In the Prep school the rules are a little more restrictive. But every boarding house has to provide a pay phone that is readily available to all the pupils and there are also phones around the school so if a child wishes to make a phone call home there is nothing to stop him or her doing that.

As I have stressed before, the pastoral care of the children was paramount. As a child I had wanted to go to boarding school, but I missed home enormously during the first two or three days of my first term and just occasionally at other times. So I was in a position to understand the feelings of children when they started boarding. Many of the children who came to our house had been boarding for a year or two already so settled very quickly. Whether they had or not, all the staff attached to the house were very sensitive to the needs of those who were new to us. We always allocated 'shadows' to the new pupils. These were boys who had been in the house for a term or two and their task, as the name implies, was to keep close to the new pupil, show him round and generally make his early days as easy as possible.

Small boys are an endearing species, but they are often untidy and grubby. One of the Matron's main tasks, supervised by Gill, was to keep an eye on their appearance and personal hygiene. Clothes were changed on a regular basis. From time to time suits would have to go to the cleaners. Before they could be sent pockets had to be emptied. There was no knowing what would be found in these. I noted on one occasion what we found in the pockets of one boy's jacket. The list, unbelievably, is as follows:

114

Two letters

A Help the Police card

French prep

Glasses and case

10 pens and pencils

3 small bottles

2 Pen refils, one full and one empty

One padlock and chain

One screwdriver

One piece of blotting paper

One key ring and key

One part of a compass

One ball-bearing and holder

One eraser

One inhaler

Six and a bit conkers

One pair of nail cutters in a case

One bootlace (knotted for conkers) with two sticky sweets on the end

One comb

Personal hygiene was something that some of the boys were reluctant to get involved in. Interestingly those who lived overseas, usually in warm climates, were keener on soap and water than some of the homebred variety! Every morning when they got up and every evening before going to bed, the boys were expected to wash and do their teeth. Occasional spot checks to see if the face flannel or toothbrush was dry would reveal a reluctance on the part of some of the boys to take their ablutions seriously! But even this method of detection wasn't foolproof as those who were really anti-washing were not past simply wetting the flannel in the hope that 'Authority' would be deceived!

Every night around ten-thirty or eleven Gill or I would do a round of the dormitories to make sure all was well. We would switch the light on, but the children rarely stirred. On one of these occasions we spied a light under the door of one of the lavatories which was on the half landing, a few steps down from the nearest dormitory. The boy who was in there had obviously heard us and waited for us to go away. However we were more patient than he was and eventually he appeared looking somewhat sheepish. We asked him if he was all right and with an affirmative answer he scuttled off back to bed. However we were convinced something wasn't quite right and so we checked the lavatory and there, under the linoleum, and not too well hidden, was a copy of Playboy or some similar magazine! He had had a good read, but I think he was a little worried, particularly when next morning he discovered that his magazine had gone. As I remember it we didn't take the matter any further. It was after all part of growing up.

Not too long after we were married we felt that a video recorder would be a useful acquisition for the House, particularly so that we could choose the Saturday entertainment for the boys rather than depend on what was provided by the normal programme schedule. Funds didn't run to this, so it was decided to do a sponsored run. However I wasn't happy about simply raising money for ourselves. It was decided that we should raise money for children with leukemia (Gill was involved with just such a charity) as well. Any money we collected was to be split fifty-fifty. The day nominated for the event duly arrived. The boys were, not surprisingly, enthusiastic. They were to run round the block just next to the House. One lap was approximately a third of a mile and the boys were sponsored for the number of laps they did. Gill felt, especially as some of the money was going to her pet charity, that she should take part. Even she would not describe herself as fleet of foot, and she had done no training, but she was determined. As small boys kept going past her she became even more determined to achieve a respectable number of laps. After running two laps (the original summit of her ambition) she did a third, then a fourth and so on. Eventually she completed 16 – over five miles! No-one was more surprised than Gill herself, although some of her sponsors were slightly shocked at how much they had to pay out!

Gill and I felt that it was important that we and the other staff were always accessible. For this reason the door to the 'Private Side' of the house was kept open at all times except at night. It was only closed then because of fire regulations. We also encouraged our staff to leave their doors open too. However as we had two dogs for most of the time we were in Hankey's it was necessary to have a baby gate, so that they couldn't wander. Sadie and Charlie gave us an enormous amount of pleasure. Sadie was our first-born. She was a black Labrador, highly intelligent and she appeared to understand everything, but only did what she wanted. She also had a rather supercilious air about her. She was a year or two older than Charlie, an orange roan Cocker, who was probably the dog equivalent of a dumb blonde. Sadie used to sit by the baby gate during prep. All would be silent as the boys set about their academic tasks. All of a sudden, without any warning, there would be a sharp bark as if to say, "No-one is taking any notice of me."

During Sadie's early days the boys used to play with her in the back garden. A great time was had by all, but we became quite worried as Sadie would seem to get over-excited and bite everything in sight. It wasn't vicious, but she had sharp little teeth. Eventually we realised that we needed to discourage the boys from getting her over-excited.

She developed into a lovely dog and she was always very good with the boys. Her greatest fault was her love of food, so much so that following an assault on a bowl of satsumas one Christmas time (the peel was left fairly neatly on the doormat) our fruit bowl in the kitchen had to be suspended from the ceiling out of her reach.

Occasionally our efforts to keep her from gorging herself failed. Some parents of one of the day boys gave us a large and very rich fruit cake wrapped in foil. I was looking forward very much to munching my way through it. We put it on a high shelf out of her reach - we were wrong! When we were out of sight she managed somehow to reach the cake and devoured every last crumb and some of the foil. She wasn't very well for the next two days and the air in her vicinity was anything but pure! Another time when she was let out into the garden last thing at night we only discovered too late that one of the boys had left the garden gate open. This was her opportunity to check the neighbourhood's bins. We searched for two hours. Although we met up with a Water Board emergency team a couple of times there was no sign of Sadie. Foxes we saw, but no dogs answering Sadie's description. We reluctantly decided there was no more that could be done and were just about to retire to bed when who should come waddling in through the garden gate, but the errant dog herself, considerably larger and heavier.

Another time when Sadie's passion for food got the better of her was when she found some silver-wrapped chocolate biscuits in the dining room. This room was rather out of the way, but occasionally boys used it as somewhere they could practice their musical instruments in relative peace and without disturbing the rest of the house community too much. Gill had a meeting later that day and had prepared a tray so she could dispense coffee and biscuits when she hosted the meeting. Unfortunately the door to the room was left open by our young musician and Sadie, who always had an eye to the main chance, not only located the biscuits, but also managed to tip the tray so that the biscuits slid off it on to the floor. When it was realised what had happened there was the worry that although the chocolate biscuits might not do her much harm the silver paper which had also been consumed might. With the help of my

CHARLIE'S DOGGONE LUCKY!

Spaniel survives 250 ft fall

By Ben Barber

CHARLIE the cocker spaniel had a miraculous escape after falling 250 feet on to Bristol's Portway.

His owners, Mr Colin Millar, and his wife Gill, were walking Charlie and their other dog, Sadie, on the Downs.

"Charlie just suddenly darted through a hole in the fence and disappeared over the edge," said Mr Millar, a Clifton College housemaster.

"We drove down to the bottom of the Portway to try to find him, but there was no sign of him, so we called the police.

"After about an hour-and-a-half, boys from the school said a lady had found Charlie on the Portway and brought him back.

"We took him to a vet, but he had no broken bones. Only a little gash and a bit of a limp. He seems to be getting better already," said Mr Millar of Cecil Road, Bristol.

Charlie and owners Colin and Gill Millar yesterday.

Charlie's claim to fame

118

House Tutor we attempted to pour quantities of salt water down Sadie's throat. That had no effect. So then a panicky phone call was made to the vet who suggested washing soda should be administered. This too seemed to be lapped up with what almost amounted to relish. So finally we gave up and hoped that her constitution was up to it. It was.

Charlie spent his early days in a baby's play pen in my study. Consequently a number of boys beat a fairly regular path to the study to see him. His claim to fame was a death-defying leap over the Avon Gorge. When this happened he was still quite young, probably about six months. It was undoubtedly his youth that saved him. We were walking the dogs along a path by the edge of the gorge. He was following a particularly good smell. Unfortunately it led him through a hole in the safety fence that had probably been made by climbers as it was a favourite spot for rock-climbing practice. The last we saw were his back legs disappearing over the cliff edge. We grabbed Sadie to make sure she didn't follow, and then I climbed over the fence and tried to peer over the edge. But it was sheer and all I could say was that I didn't think we would be seeing Charlie again alive.

Although we had no hope of seeing Charlie again alive, we had to see if we could find his body. Having delivered Sadie back to the House, we set out for the spot where we thought Charlie would have fallen. Appropriately enough it was near a Hot Dog Stand at the foot of the Gorge. Of Charlie there was no sign. By now it was raining. In desperation we phoned the police. Two policemen arrived and they were charming. We wondered if Charlie had lodged on a ledge. Could a climber perhaps attempt a search? "Oh no!" the police said. "In this weather they wouldn't attempt to climb for a human being let alone a dog." The police could offer no help, only comfort. Further search still revealed no sign of Charlie. We were cold and wet so it seemed time to take Gill home. I was then going to return for one last look. But as we were driving home we spotted three boys from the House who had come to find us to tell us that Charlie had been found and delivered back to Hankey's. Poor little Charlie, he was wet and dirty and more dead than alive. He had a small gash in his head and a gammy back leg. However a trip to the vet assured us that he had no broken bones. The prognosis was that if the shock didn't kill him he should survive.

Although we normally never allowed the dogs to sleep in the bedroom, this time we made an exception to the rule. During the night we seemed to listen to his every breath, terrified that he might stop breathing. The daytime was spent in his bed in the kitchen. A week went by. There was some improvement, but still he hardly stirred out of his bed. One morning it was obvious Sadie thought he had had enough attention and that he should start living again. So she went over to him and more or less nudged him out of bed. Charlie had recovered!

There were a number of repercussions from this event. We were quite keen to find out who had picked Charlie up so we could thank them. But the person who had delivered him back at Hankey's had not left a name. So I wrote a letter to the local evening paper, the Evening Post. It turned out that a lorry driver who had been taking a short cut home had picked him up as he struggled across the Portway. The Portway, for those unfamiliar with Bristol, is a main and fast road that follows the Avon through the Avon Gorge and links Avonmouth, Bristol's port, to the City of Bristol. How Charlie evaded the traffic we shall never know. But evade it he did. The lorry driver gave him to a lady who had a Morris Traveller, and it was she who brought him to Hankey's. We located the lorry driver, but never found out who the lady with the Morris Traveller was. Although we didn't meet the lorry driver, who incidentally owned a spaniel himself, we went to his home and left a bottle of whisky for him as a mark of our appreciation. We also left a bottle of whisky at the local police station for the two policemen who had been so sympathetic.

At this time Gill didn't drive. Some weeks later she was returning home from the local supermarket on her new bicycle with the food shopping. She was over-laden. There were bags on the front, the back and swinging from the handlebars. As she rode along the road, somewhat tentatively and probably not in total control, a police car pulled up and the window was wound down. Gill was now distinctly worried, but having got off her bicycle she was greeted not with a reprimand, but a smiling face. It was the policemen who had assisted us when Charlie did his death-defying leap. They had just stopped to say thank you for the bottle of whisky! Gill breathed a huge sigh of relief when they drove off.

The dogs weren't the only animals attached to Hankey's. Outside in the yard was the pet shed. This housed an assortment of small animals - mainly gerbils, hamsters and a white rat which had a habit of escaping and hiding underneath the shed. There were frequent dramas associated with these animals, but the one that we will always remember concerned Muddy. During the first summer term after Gill and I were married I was approached by Nutty, Muddy's owner, and a group of his friends, who asked that they might be allowed to let Muddy mate. The only problem was that it had to be done after dusk which was about the time the boys went to bed. So at about 10.00pm four or five of the boys came down in their pyjamas and dressing gowns. Muddy was brought in from the pet shed together with a suitable male. One boy stood by with a milk bottle full of cold water not so much to dampen their ardour, but because, so we were assured, once the hamsters had mated, the female was likely to attack her mate or even kill him. The mating process appeared to go on for at least twenty minutes and seemed anything but loving and gentle. By this time we were all fairly exhausted and although Muddy showed no signs of wanting to devour her mate we felt that enough was enough. For Gill, who had had no brothers and therefore little experience of small boys, the evening was quite an eye-opener!

Sadly the story of Muddy did not have a happy ending. The night before Sports Day, which was about the time Muddy was due to deliver, her owner came to see me to say that Muddy was not very well. Indeed she was very bloated. We decided to wait and see how things were in the morning. Morning came and Muddy was discovered on her back with her feet in the air. She was dead. Being Sports Day we were all rushing round in a frantic state, but it was important to try and console Nutty. So we arranged a short burial service. Muddy was buried with suitable ceremony and a headstone made of wood with the words "Muddy died in Childbirth Sports Day 1976" was placed by the grave.

Clifton College first opened its doors in 1862, but it wasn't till 1987 that the school first took in girls. Girls generally did not figure much in the lives of our boys in Hankeys's. Although, particularly in the summer terms, one or two girls could occasionally be seen loitering round the boys' entrance of Hankey's. In an effort to regularize this – I wasn't too happy about the boys and girls hanging around the street for long periods – we tried to encourage the boys to bring the girls into the house. This didn't really work and in the end the boys and girls would wander round to a nearby sports field where they could be seen sitting in a circle on the cricket square chatting away contentedly.

The decision to take girls was heralded as socially and educationally sound, but it happened at a time when boarding numbers in independent schools generally were taking a huge dive. No doubt economic considerations played a part as well. There were only a handful of girls to begin with in 1987. Even those few threw some of the staff into a state of panic. Changing the culture of an all-boys school to a mixed one did not come easily. Most of the men on the staff regarded girls as inherently good, gentle and sensitive, whereas boys were naughty and needed to be kept up to the mark. It took some of the male staff a long time, even years, to realise that girls could be every bit as naughty as boys and often more devious!

Girls were regarded as good and sensitive,
whereas boys were naughty and needed to be kept up to the mark
Contemporary cartoon by the Art Master (Peter Clay)

122

Chapter 14 – Odds and Ends

The Chapel was still a focal point of school life despite the fact that in latter years the Pre only worshipped there three or, at most, four times a term - a far cry from when I was a boy at school when we went every Sunday and sometimes twice. The building itself is lovely and has one or two features of note. Firstly, the congregation faced inwards – not of course unheard of, but unusual. When the chapel was enlarged in 1912 extra lighting was provided by a hexagonal lantern in the centre. At the east end of the building the windows designed in the 1930s by Hugh Easton provide a blaze of colour. The west end has a more delicate rose window. This is partially hidden from inside the Chapel by the magnificent Harrison organ. But from the outside on a dark winter's evening when the lights are on inside the effect is magical. One other treasure tucked away in a small side chapel is a mosaic by Holman Hunt of the Light of the World fame. Although we were not a Choir School, we traditionally maintained a high standard of music. The services were geared to the children and were if not enjoyed by all the children at least tolerated. I personally looked forward to them. With large congregations, singing loud enough to drown my sometimes less than tuneful efforts and sermons that were usually fairly brief and often entertaining, the services were enjoyable.

Two services in the year were particularly exciting and required rehearsals and numerous choir practices to make sure that they went without a hitch. One I have already mentioned was the Commemoration Service and the other was the Carol Service usually on the last Thursday of the Christmas Term. This was always a moving occasion. The choir was always in tip top form. It seemed to grow in size for this service. Not only were additional children drafted in to swell the numbers, but also the number of adults especially men increased significantly. The climax of the service came towards the end. All the lights went out and the chapel was enveloped in darkness. Then, as an introduction to a reading telling of the birth of Christ, a procession of candle carriers came into the chapel. As the candle carriers spread to all parts of the chapel, so the building filled with light, to symbolize Christ as The Light of the World. This was made particularly poignant by the fact that the carriers were the youngest and smallest in the school. They would enter in a very slow procession with studied concentration, as they attempted, usually successfully, but not always, to maintain the gap between them and the next person; and also to keep the candle upright and not, in the darkness, trip over any steps they might have to negotiate. The children with their faces lit up by the candles they were carrying looked angelic.

Chapel brings back one particular memory for quite the wrong reason. Gill's mother had come to live in 'Sheltered Accomodation' in Bristol, and she loved coming to the services. On one never-to-be-forgotten occasion she came and towards the end of the service she passed out. In the panic I could not recollect which of the parents in the congregation were doctors so I beetled over to the Headmaster who had just completed his sermon and had resumed his seat in the centre of the building. He pointed me in the direction of a parent, who was a doctor. I rushed over to him and he, in turn, came over to where my mother-in-law was now lying on the pew. Fortunately we were seated at the back so we were reasonably inconspicuous. He examined her briefly and then said, so quietly that I didn't hear, "I think she's gone!" After he repeated what he had said so I could hear as well as a much larger audience of parents and children I set off to call for an ambulance. But now the service was drawing to a close and the choir was proceeding out. I wove my way through them totally oblivious to them and everyone else. I was just concentrating on my need to find a telephone as quickly as possible. As I waited for the ambulance an eminent surgeon who was known to me, and who had been singing in the choir, enquired as to what had been going on. On being informed he went back to see my poor mother-in-law and then returned to say that Mother, surrounded by doctors, was sitting up and seemed to be OK!

At the time we had thought it was an appropriate send off - complete with choir if not perhaps with heavenly angels. Happily Gill's mother survived that scare and lived on another eight or ten years to the ripe old age of 91.

With a generous food allowance I felt it incumbent on me to do a fair amount of entertaining. Food for Christmas parties was provided by the central school kitchens. One such party I remember had to take place in the School dining rooms as Gill was recovering from major surgery. She could not possibly have organized the meal herself, but did not wish to miss the party so we arranged that a couple of the school buses, used for transporting children to our sports fields on the other side of the Avon, should pick us up. These were large with doors opening in the middle and with lots of standing room. Duly the buses arrived and we were transported the 400yards to the school dining room. In fact the driver did a detour to make the journey more worth while! After the meal we returned by bus to Hankey's to finish the evening off with the normal programme of silly games.

Other entertaining included a number of 'Lobster Balls'. This was the name given to the low key 'knees up' that we usually had at the end of Lobster Week, the week after the end of term when the Pre Staff cricket team played many of their matches. It involved not much more than plenty of beer and wine plus bread and cheese and a record player. It was attended by most of the Lobsters and quite a number of their opponents. One year a couple of the local constabulary appeared. I think they came to inform us that they had had a complaint about the noise, which I don't really remember being too dreadful. Anyway they joined us in a beer and then slipped away with our assurances that we would turn the volume down.

One other party that stands out was my 50th. I knew something was happening but I didn't know quite what. Gill had organised it and I wasn't involved at all. Someone else was on duty so all I had to do was enjoy the party. We had food and drink, dancing in the library and then at midnight a cake was brought in by the boys all in their dressing gowns and pyjamas. They all came down except one and after the candle lighting and blowing out ceremony they joined in the dancing for a short while before being packed off to bed again. The boy who missed the party was very upset – he had slept through everything!

Little has been said about teaching in these pages. Teaching, of course, played a huge part in my life and although when I was a Housemaster I felt that the pastoral side was the most important aspect of my work. Nevertheless classroom work could not be neglected. After all, sadly perhaps, most schools are probably largely judged firstly on what they provide in the classroom. Over the years I have turned a hand to English, Mathematics, Latin and Science, as well as Geography, the subject I studied at University. In the late

1960s I was sent off to a Malvern Science course with a view to introducing Science into the Pre. The philosophy behind the course was that teachers and pupils should learn together. I learnt extremely quickly!

As Clifton Prep is a large school by Prep School standards most staff taught their own subject and in the latter years I taught Geography almost exclusively. The big bonus of teaching Geography is that most children seem to enjoy the subject. It was not difficult to keep them interested. In my early days at Clifton there was a small boy who had a glass eye. He sat at the front of the class and when he was bored he would get out a pencil and tap his glass eye. I am glad to say I wasn't subjected to this treatment!

I suppose the downside of teaching Geography was that it required much preparation and a considerable amount of marking.

A number of times during the early 1970s we took the whole school on expeditions on the old paddle steamer the Balmoral. As these trips had a Geographical bias it fell to me to organize these trips. This necessitated getting two or three hundred children and assorted staff on to a fleet of buses and down to the embarkation point. Embarkation depended to some extent on the tide. On one occasion we embarked from the lock by the big swing bridge not too far from the school. Another time we embarked at Avonmouth, some seven miles from the centre of Bristol. Here the tides are the second highest in the world so the timing of the trip was fairly critical. In the hope that the children would learn something of the History, Natural History and Geography of the area questionnaires were distributed as well as a fairly large amount of information. There was also a commentary. One year unfortunately it was fairly foggy and the commentary seemed to dwell rather too much on the muddiness of the water. As we couldn't see very far I suppose it did not matter too much. But the lack of excitement on deck meant that the more active children looked for alternative excitement down below! Fortunately the attempts of a small group to get behind the grill of the bar and siphon off the odd pint of beer were soon thwarted!

About a year before we left Hankey's we had decided that we should sell our cottage in the country. It had proved a very welcome bolt hole for us during our time in the school boarding house. It was now time to move on and look for something of our own in Clifton, the area where we had lived for the first ten years of our married life. The only drawback with living in this lovely suburb on the edge of Bristol is that it spoils you for anywhere else. Unfortunately a lot of other people are attracted to this area as well and houses are not cheap. But we were determined to find something. In the end and with some hesitation, we settled for a flat. We did a small amount of cosmetic work on the flat and moved some of the furniture into it from the cottage. Then one day, we went to have yet another look at it. We walked into the sitting room and were greeted by loud music being played by one of the youngsters upstairs. It was as if the record player or CD player was actually in the room that we were in. That was too much for Gill and she burst into tears. I can't say I was too happy either.

Next day the flat was put into the hands of a friendly estate agent. We never actually slept in the flat. But Gill's mother and a couple of her buddies had spent a week there. It was a sort of annual reunion. I suspect they did so much talking that they didn't notice any extraneous noises!

The flat was put on the market for roughly what we paid for it, say about £50,000. Eventually, after I had moaned to our friendly estate agent that there had been no interest shown in our property, she suggested we should put the price UP by about £10,000. I couldn't believe what I was hearing. But in a few days we had a nibble and in no time at all the flat was sold. After this slightly unfortunate experience, we decided we would wait till the following summer before we continued our search for the "house of our dreams". Then one day when Gill was looking in an estate agents window in a fairly desultory way she spotted just the house. It was a mews house in a road called Camp Road, which is in quiet corner of Clifton. As it turned out it was owned by someone whose son I had taught. Knowing the vendor was a bonus and she was in no rush to leave, so we did not have to complete purchase until we were ready to depart from Hankey's at the end of the summer term. Indeed, good to her word, she never pressed us to speed up the process of signing contract although her new house was ready for occupancy earlier than she had expected. We were very fortunate.

The House was just right for us except it had a minute garden. However it did have a small patio which I later enlarged and this did face south - critical from Gill's point of view. The house had been converted from stables into a house some twenty-five years earlier. When we moved in July 1986 we received a delightful card from the wife of the man who had been headmaster at the time I returned from Canada. She was from an old Bristol family and she explained that as a young girl she had lived in one of the 'Big houses' on the Promenade but that she had been allowed to play in Camp Road. She said that in the early days she used to love watching the grooms as they brushed their horses and polished the brasses. Then things changed and stables became garages. The horses and carriages gave way to Daimlers. The grooms became chauffeurs and they turned their hands to polishing their cars. Eventually many of the garages became houses.

It goes without saying that during the fifteen years that I had lived in Hankey's I had accumulated a fair amount of furniture as well as huge amounts of what can only be described as rubbish. Nevertheless, wherever we moved, it was unlikely that there would be room for all our possessions. Indeed some of them would be simply too big. So the lovely huge mahogany linen chest and one or two other large items were sold by auction. Most of the rest went to a car boot sale. This was an unforgettable experience. We had never attended one of these functions before and naively thought they were a simple way of getting rid of our unwanted possessions. They were certainly a way of getting rid of them, though not quite in the manner we had envisaged. We paid our £5 entry fee at the gate to the field where the sale was being held and drove to an empty space. As we came to a standstill the car was surrounded by people in a somewhat menacing manner. We emerged from the car and went round to open the back. As we did so the crowd surged forward, every one of them anxious to have first option on anything that we might produce. As we pulled out the boxes, and then, unwrapped the various items they contained, hands would stretch through as if laying claim. There was a barrage of questions asking how much we wanted for this item or that. We needed eyes in the back of our head. How much slipped away without our knowledge I do not know. When just about everything had gone - most items paid for -we packed up the few remaining useless bits and pieces and returned to Hankey's vowing never to go to a car boot sale again.

It is very difficult, for those who have never experienced it, to appreciate just how running a boarding house can take over one's life. I believed that the children in our care were an extended family. Sometimes quite little things could be very important in the eyes of a small boy. I remember returning to the house one Sunday after we had been out for a few hours and there was a little chap waiting for us even as we opened the front door. "Sir," he said, "May I, on Sunday week, wear my rough stuff when I go out with my parents?" It may seem insignificant, but he had obviously been worrying about this and had been waiting most of the afternoon for us to return so he could ask the question.

Inevitably we came to know most of the boys very well. When they moved on to the Senior School or elsewhere we often kept in touch. But those same boys who we knew as open friendly individuals in Hankey's often found adolescence difficult to handle. Adolescence can be likened to going through a tunnel. I have known boys fifteen years of age, on seeing Gill or myself, cross over to the other side of the road to avoid contact. It was very hurtful. Yet, those same boys, two or three years later, spying us in the distance, would go out of their way to come and say, "Hello!"

One Christmas Eve, many years later, we were walking home from a dinner party, when we saw a slightly scruffy-looking individual, in a dark jacket and woolly hat. It was late at night, so I thought it would be a good idea if we crossed over to the other side of the road to ensure there was no chance of a confrontation. Suddenly a cheerful voice shouted out, "Hello Sir! Hello Gill!" The slightly scruffy individual was an ex-pupil. Being much younger than us he was heading to a party and, not like us, from one. We exchanged pleasantries and parted with the words, "See you in Chapel tomorrow!"

Chapter 15 - Sabbatical

Our departure from Hankey's was, inevitably, sad. I had been Housemaster for just over 15 years and I had had Gill's assistance for 10 of those years. I had been there from just after its inception, and when we left it was a thriving concern, although the building itself was ready for a face lift. It was somewhat ironic that as soon as we moved out full central heating was installed.

Before we left Hankey's I had been appointed Second Master, but I was granted a Sabbatical Term before starting my duties.

The highlight of our sabbatical term was a six week round-the- world trip, which took us to Canada via Amsterdam, to Hawaii, Australia, Bali, Thailand and Hong Kong. One of the advantages of living and working in a boarding school is that you meet people from different parts of the globe. Some of these contacts made our trip much more interesting than it might otherwise have been.

We embarked on our world trip at the beginning of November 1986. In all we took off and landed fifteen times, but only one flight was late and that, as luck would have it, was the very first one. Most of our journey was in the Southern Hemisphere or the tropics, so the Canadian leg of the journey was the only time when we were going to need warm clothes. In anticipation of this we had packed one case with warm clothes. After the delayed start we arrived at Schipol in Amsterdam with barely half an hour to spare before our next flight was due to leave. As we hurried along endless corridors, we wondered if we ourselves, let alone the luggage, would make the connection. We eventually arrived at the place where our on-going flight was waiting, but when we reached Ottawa one piece of luggage was missing - it was, of course, the bag containing the warm clothes! As we had a five or six hour wait in Ottawa I had arranged to see some friends from my Shawnigan Lake days. They whisked us off to their home for supper. By nine pm we were overwhelmed by tiredness. We had left home at about 7.00 am UK time. Ottawa is five hours behind us, so at 9.00 pm in Ottawa our personal time-clocks said it was 2.00 am in the morning. We were quite ready to get back on a plane again for the flight to Vancouver and the opportunity to catch up on some sleep. Incidentally our mislaid luggage caught up with us as we flew out of Vancouver three or four days later!

The Canadian part of the trip was, of course, simply an excuse to catch up with old friends. It was lovely to see Jim and Hilda, who were part of the original Cliffside set-up and also Derek and Mary. Derek was a Housemaster at Shawnigan Lake School which you might describe as the school that spawned Cliffside. Derek was a keen sportsman and taught PE and games. He and I played cricket and rugby together with local clubs. It was with him I used to watch the 'Football' on New Year's Day. His wife Mary, who had a lovely infectious laugh, was constantly trying to find me a suitable wife!

Our flight to Canada from Schipol had been notable for one other reason. When we found our allotted seats in the plane, I discovered that I was sitting next to a lady of East European extraction of enormous proportions. She simply overflowed her seat. We were so wedged in that when she laughed I had to laugh with her. Late in the journey she decided to take a trip to the toilets at the rear of the plane. Eventually she managed to extricate herself and waded down the aisle like a tidal wave. I breathed a sigh of relief, but she was soon back. On her return however it was necessary to wedge her back into her seat and it appeared she could not do this unassisted. The arms of her seat had to be raised and then when she was in her seat the armrests were forced down. Surplus rolls of flesh were then tucked in as well. She was accompanied on her journey by a small rather insignificant man who, I assume was her husband. He spoke little, but was noticeable for the fact that he kept this green pork pie type hat on his head for the whole journey. The only other remarkable thing about these two occurred at the end of the flight. Seasoned travellers will know that when the plane stops the vast majority of passengers leap to their feet in a frenzied attempt to be first away totally forgetting that in any case, they are going to have to wait at the carousel for their luggage, and that, as far as I can ascertain, is a lottery. On this occasion when the plane stopped I looked up and realised our East European friends had not only vacated their seats but were already by the exit door leading the rush to get off. Given the width of my erstwhile neighbour I still marvel at how they achieved this feat.

One of the problems of travelling long distances by air is 'Jet-lag'. We had just completed a long flight from Hawaii with a brief refuelling stop in Fiji and arrived in Sydney in the morning. We decided we shouldn't waste any time, so we went down to the quay and took a boat trip to Manley. This was fine but we were both undoubtedly scratchy and this got worse! On our return we decided to have a late lunch and then headed for our hotel where we were to stay one night before moving on. It was now late afternoon. We thought we would just have a quick nap and then get up and explore a bit more of Sydney. Unfortunately the next thing we knew it was 11.00 pm - too late to do much exploring and, in any case, by then we hadn't the energy, so we raided the fridge and went back to bed.

The only other incident of note during our actual travels occurred at Bangkok Airport. When we left Hong Kong we had been penalised as our luggage had been overweight. We were determined this shouldn't happen again. So books, photographs - we had had a large number of films developed - and heavy items were transferred to our hand luggage. We had purchased in Hong Kong a fairly light expandable bag. This was an ingenious contraption. Initially it was the size of a normal piece of hand luggage. It was constructed on the principle of a concertina. To make the bag bigger you simply unzipped one of a number of zips that ran round it. The bag was filled and it was very heavy. With this as our hand luggage, the bags that we had to check in were considerably lighter. We were fortunate. Our luggage was not over weight. However there was one nasty scare. As we were led out to the plane one of the other passengers noticed that Gill was staggering under a great weight. He very gallantly offered to take her bag. The offer was gratefully accepted. Gill, who now had very little to carry, proceeded rapidly. She had reached the top of the gangway, at which point she turned round. She saw the poor man who was carrying her luggage as well as his own had been stopped on the tarmac and engaged in conversation by one of the security staff. He was obviously being asked why he had so much hand luggage. As she watched she saw a certain amount of gesticulation and then the man pointed at Gill. Finally they appeared to part amicably and the man continued his walk to the plane. It had been a worrying moment. I think we were lucky too. I hate to think how a similar incident today might have ended.

In Hawaii and later in Bali we stayed in and enjoyed the luxury of smart hotels and were, I suppose, fairly typical tourists. Lovely though many of the places we visited were, the trip was really made by the people we met and the places we visited that we wouldn't normally have seen. There was the ex-colleague from Clifton, who was then a Headmaster of a prep school in Melbourne. He showed us round his school and then took us out of town to the school's lovely permanent campsite. In Melbourne we stayed with Janet the aunt of boys in Hankey's, who ran a rather up-market dress shop. She and Toby entertained marvellously. They also arranged for me to have lunch with a nephew of Robert Menzies at the Melbourne Club, as I believe it was called. I don't remember much about the day of the lunch except that it was one of the coldest November days on record! I arrived at the Club, which had all the appearances of a London Club - panelled walls, leather upholstered armchairs and so on. Unfortunately I had assumed that as I was in a supposedly warm country everyone would be wearing lightweight suits. I had donned a light blue suit and thought I cut a bit of a dash in it. Imagine my horror when I walked in through the door of the club and saw that every single member was dressed in a dark suit. My light weight effort stood out like a sore thumb.

After Melbourne, we returned to Sydney, where we stayed with more relations of those two boys who had been in Hankey's. Again we were regally entertained.

Hong Kong too was exciting. Here we stayed in the 'New Wing' of the YMCA. It wasn't as smart as some of the hotels, but was more than adequate. Our room had bathroom-en-suite, telephone, TV, safe and it was spotlessly clean. We had been told by parents of another boy in Hankeys to phone up when we reached Hong Kong. This we did. We were warmly greeted and invited to go with them on their boat next day. They were going out to lunch. There was hesitation on Gill's part, as she is not a good sailor and was reluctant to spend one of only four days in Hong Kong being seasick. We accepted with what I hope sounded like enthusiasm. When we reached the Yacht Club, where we were to meet, I suggested that perhaps I should find the cloakroom before we set off. The response was that there wasn't a problem as there were two loos on board! The boat was huge. We set off past the thousands of sampans that were the homes of countless citizens of Hong Kong. We eventually reached more open water. Our destination was an island that had a particularly good restaurant, where we were going to be treated to an authentic Chinese meal. As it turned out Gill's fears were groundless. The sea was calm except for the occasional wash of a sampan, barge or one of the countless little boats that plied the waters around Hong Kong.

We covered a lot of ground during our four days in Hong Kong. Then on our last night there the same people who had taken us in their boat invited us to dinner at the Peninsular Hotel, which just happened to be next door to our base. Our host, who worked with Reuters, was entertaining a correspondent from India and would we like to join them? This was a memorable evening. It was somewhat incongruous that at the end of the evening we were walked back from the luxury of the Peninsular Hotel to where we were staying - the YMCA!

Initially in Bangkok we were greeted by a brother of a friend who was building bridges in Thailand at the time. He made us very welcome and showed us around. We had had three or four Thai boys in Hankey's and their parents all in their different ways made us very welcome. One of them offered us a Grannie House at the bottom of their garden and also a chauffeur driven car. There is so much to see in Bangkok – the King's Palace, various Buddhas, and temples. But Bangkok is a city teaming with people and vehicles of every description including countless extremely noisy mopeds. The car, which had air-conditioning, not only shielded us from the heat, but also from the noise and fumes. It was a big bonus. Apart from being able to go where we wanted we did not have to worry about parking. But it is curious fact that if you are not used to having a chauffeur at your beck and call it takes a while to get used to such luxury.

And so back to our new home and work in my new role as Second Master.

Chapter 16 Life after Hankey's

The life of a Housemaster is all-consuming and so, of course, our departure from Hankey's was particularly sad. It had been our life for the first ten years of marriage. Although we had enjoyed our time there Gill and I soon realised there was another life outside the House and never once did we regret leaving. We were suddenly faced with a freedom that we had forgotten existed. We had had a good innings and it was now time to move on. The commitment and the fact that you really are involved 24 hours a day, seven days a week make the job rewarding, but hard work and stressful. It was a forgotten experience to go home at the end of the day, no matter how late, and to be able to close the door and more or less forget about work till next morning. Although my new job as Deputy Head kept me busy, when I was away from school, my time was my own. Some times in those days soon after leaving Hankey's we would drive past the House at say 9.30 pm and give silent thanks that we weren't chasing up the reluctant washers, putting the boys to bed and making sure the house was reasonably tidy before doing any other things that required doing.

I was once asked to write a small piece for a magazine for schoolteachers titled, 'The Life in the Day of a Deputy Headmaster'. This proved quite difficult because no two days are the same and the job by its very nature almost defies description. There are of course many strands. One deputy described his main role as being a favourable interpreter of the Headmaster's latest unpopular edict. Acting as a liaison officer between the Head and his staff was certainly one role. For one year during my spell as Deputy, my Head was Chairman of the IAPS. This is a professional association for Heads of independent preparatory schools world wide. The aim of the association is to promote all-round excellence in education in its widest sense. Because my headmaster was inevitably away a lot on IAPS business more work came my way. It was even more essential that I provided the communication links between him and the staff. One of the first things I did each morning was to see him to confirm he was going to be in school that day, to discuss any current problems and to see if there were any tasks that I needed to do on his behalf if he was away.

I found the days busy and because it was a very different job from being a Housemaster I attacked it with renewed enthusiasm. Although I shared an office I was still able to shut myself away, if necessary, to get on with administrative work. Also because my administrative load was heavier my teaching commitments were reduced slightly.

One of the most tedious jobs I had to do was to arrange cover for those who couldn't take their lessons for what ever reasons. It is surprising how many lessons require cover even in a term when illness is not a big factor. Usually reasons were genuine and involved not only staff who were ill, but those going on courses, taking teams away, the occasional wedding or funeral and so on. Inevitably there were always those who seemed to ask for cover more than others. The only time I was really put out was when a member of staff reported ill in the morning and was then spotted at the opera later that day - a very rapid recovery! Colleagues were press-ganged into covering. Most accepted the request to cover if not with enthusiasm certainly with good grace. But there were always those who couldn't possibly help as they were much too busy. It is ironic, but generally those who were busiest were the ones who were quickest to volunteer.

There were dozens of other things that needed doing such as helping with the interviewing of new staff, and, when new staff came to the school helping to make them feel welcome and to integrate into their new environment, interviewing children for scholarships, reading up on recent educational legislation, dealing with any discipline problems, putting in an appearance at matches and, especially if the HM wasn't around, talking to parents, supervising lunch, taking assembly, and meeting my opposite number in the Senior School to exchange ideas and discuss any mutual problems. In general I suppose you could say the main role of a Deputy Headmaster was that of a troubleshooter. The list is almost unending, but one thing I did not do was the timetable. For that I was grateful. It was a particularly unenviable task as it was complicated by the fact that sports, and some other facilities, were shared with the Senior School and our timetables didn't really dove-tail.

Now two Deputy Heads do what I did and much more. One has responsibility for dealing with parents (they are considerably more demanding these days), keeping abreast of Key Stage 2, organizing exams and so on. The other is more involved with pastoral care, Health and Safety which includes fire practices and punishments. The two Deputies with the Headmaster make up the Management Team. Another member of staff deals with that most exercising of tasks – the timetable.

One of my more pleasant tasks was to host a small drinks party at the end of each term. These were really an opportunity to thank staff and particularly any staff who might be retiring or leaving and moving on elsewhere. I am not a natural speaker so although I enjoyed preparing for these occasions they did not come easily to me.

In 1993 with the departure of one Head in April to fresh pastures and the arrival of a new one in September I was asked to fill in during the summer term. With some trepidation, I accepted. But as things turned out this was a very exciting and fulfilling period and with hindsight one I wouldn't have missed for the worlds.

It was customary for the Head to preach once during each term and I felt I should do the same. During my sermon which was basically about being considerate to others, I let it be known that it was normal practice for Gill to mark sermons out of ten! My main concern was that I should receive a reasonable mark. Inevitably when I left the Chapel many of the parents suggested what mark I merited. Those who knew me well offered a mere one or two, and those who knew me less well and wanting perhaps to keep me sweet suggested 9 or 10!

During the course of this sermon I told a story that had always been a favourite of mine. It is worth repeating here as it illustrates what I believe to be one of the most important philosophies of life.

A Chieftain from a primitive tribe dreamed that he died and the angels came to take him to a place where he would be happy for always. But he was worried about those of his people who were doomed to be miserable, and asked whether he might go to see these unfortunate ones.

"Yes", said the angels, and they took him to a place where the skies were blue, the sun shone and the buildings were beautiful and bright. He was taken into a hall where there were tables laden with all kinds of lovely foods.

"But," said the chieftain, "how can the people here be miserable? This is a delightful place." The angel told him, "There is one rule here that must not be broken. The food can only be eaten with chop-sticks five foot long." Then the chieftain realized why the people were suffering agonies of hunger with all that lovely food in front of them.

Feeling a little sad, he was taken by the angel to the place of happiness. There too the skies were blue, the sun shone and the buildings were beautiful and bright. He was taken into a hall where the tables were laden with delicious food.

"But this is exactly like the other place," he said, "except that the people here look happy and contented. I suppose there is no rule here about chop-sticks?"

"Oh yes, there is," replied the angel. "The food can only be eaten with chop-sticks five foot long."

"How is it, then, that the people here are happy?" asked the chieftain.

"Here," the angel replied, "the people have learned to feed each other."

At Commemoration, which occurs in the middle of the summer term, along with the Chairman of Council and the President, I had to speak to the parents and children – an audience of well over fifteen hundred. The sermon had been relatively straight forward as I simply had to find a topic that I felt strongly about. The Commem speech was more difficult. My position as Headmaster was only temporary and therefore I was not involved in School policy-making, so I couldn't really discuss the future of the school. Instead I opted to talk about what had been achieved by the children, but I took as my general theme, the speed of change since I arrived at Clifton as a still fairly small boy of eleven years in April 1945.

I finished with these words. 'I was reminded recently of a small boy whose report arrived at home. He knew it wasn't very good so he took it to his father and said, "Before you read this, Dad, would you please dig out one of your reports and read that."

Although children now grow up more quickly than they did in 1945, I think sometimes we forget what it is like to be young. The demands on them, I believe, are greater than ever today. Just as that small boy who started at boarding school in 1945 needed encouragement and understanding from his parents, so today, nearly half a century later, your children need the same understanding and encouragement – that is something that doesn't change. Schools are not factories. We can do our best not only in the classroom teaching the 3 Rs, but also outside it, teaching the difference between right and wrong and trying to broaden horizons. But it is essential that schools and parents work in partnership. Only that way will we get the best out of your children.'

I felt privileged to have been asked to step in as Acting Head for a term. But I also counted myself very lucky on several counts. Firstly I was extremely fortunate to be offered such an exciting opportunity, and secondly that I should have had such wonderful support from staff, children, the Bursar and the Headmaster of the Upper School.

It is a curious fact that year groups have a character which can distinguish them from other year groups. The Year 8s, that is the children in their last year at the Pre, this particular year were fun, but were also an extremely lively lot. They were growing out of the Pre and beginning to flex their muscles. So very early in term I assembled them and asked for their cooperation, stressing the need to make it a fun term for all of us. In this respect they played their part admirably.

The staff, as I have already said, couldn't have been more supportive. One of the most difficult decisions a Head has to make is whether or not to ask parents to remove their child from the school. I found myself in this situation. Having been expelled from a school myself, I suppose I was in a better position than many to appreciate this. The child concerned undoubtedly had problems which the departing Headmaster had already discussed with the parents. The child had been to see a psychologist, but we had reached the end of the line there as the next step would have been for the parents themselves to visit the psychologist and this they refused to do. I had to assess how much harm he was doing to other children and to the general morale of the school, and weigh this against how much we could help the child involved. In the end I had no doubt at all that the decision to tell the parents that their son could not return after half term was the right one. I was increasingly aware of the effect this child was having on the other children, especially the girls. The encouragement I received from the staff in this matter was vital. I was also supported by the Bursar, the Head of the Senior School and the school council. This was despite the fact that owing to the recession, Clifton, like most independent schools at the time was finding it hard to maintain their numbers and the boy in question had two siblings. It was likely that they would be withdrawn as well.

Most Heads these days simply don't have enough hours in the day to spend much time in the classroom, although as I have already indicated if it is possible to squeeze in a few lessons a week it is, I am certain, of benefit to both the children and the Head himself. Curiously one of the problems for me during my inter-regnum term was not so much insufficient time, but the need to change mode, for want of a better expression. If I had been to a Council Meeting or some other meeting where there had been a surge of adrenalin it was quite difficult to then come back to teaching a normal lesson.

The in-coming Headmaster had some equally difficult decisions to make during his first term. Because of falling pupil numbers it became necessary to make a number of staff redundant. I had hinted that this might happen at a Staff Meeting in the summer term, but few colleagues seemed to take his on board. Inevitably perhaps there was the feeling that it won't happen to us. The School Council, however, was adamant and redundancies became a reality. Perhaps it was a good thing that the task of nominating those who should leave should fall to the new Head on the grounds that being new to the school he had no emotional ties with any of the staff and could tackle the problem more objectively. Be that as it may it was a hugely difficult exercise and one that stirred up the emotions and passions of many of the staff. It was a fiery baptism for a new Headmaster. Nor was it made any easier by the death of two apparently healthy colleagues within a few weeks of each other early in his term of office. The morale of the staff which was already low sank to new depths. The children too were devastated and somehow the staff had to be strong so they could support the children.

I suppose from that low point one of the Head's main priorities must have been to rebuild Staff morale. Over the last fifty years I have worked with a number of very different headmasters. All have been people at the top of their profession. But it has been fascinating to me to observe, especially since I have been at the Pre, the particular strengths of the different heads.

I do not know what the new Head's brief was. It may have included improving the fabric of the school. But he also felt very strongly about the need to curb bullying - not that it was any more of a problem than in any other school. Indeed it was probably less of a problem than in most. Bullying takes so many forms and is so complex that it is almost impossible to eradicate completely. The first question to ask is, "At what point does gentle teasing become bullying?" It is a sad fact that some people by their very nature invite bullying upon themselves. Curiously it is not necessarily those who have a physical defect that come in for unkind treatment. I remember one particular boy who had very real problems walking. He had a number of operations to try to alleviate this, but he always had a pronounced limp and couldn't move very fast. Despite this he was very keen on rugby and usually liked to play scrum half where he felt in the thick of it all. His guts and determination to make light of his difficulties, and his personality, ensured that the other boys rarely, if ever, teased him. Nevertheless the more that children can be made aware of what bullying is, what it feels like to be bullied, and the more an anti-bullying culture can be established, the better.

The last time I used a gym shoe in anger, and that was probably some twenty-five years ago, was on a boy who had been bullying one of the smaller members of the house. In today's climate that may be deemed to be the wrong thing to do. However I still feel the use of corporal punishment as a last sanction is a useful weapon.

I consider myself very fortunate that when I stepped down as Deputy Head I was offered an administrative post. I took on two of the smaller tasks that I had been doing as Deputy Head, namely arranging cover for absent staff and keeping an attendance record. But my main role was to keep tabs on the Pre teaching budget and to liaise with the main accounts office, which was in a building on the other side of the campus.

Chapter 17 – Final Thoughts

I wonder to myself whether these are the ramblings of someone who has had his day. It is so easy to say, "Things aren't what they were in my day." It may well be that young teachers of today who know no different see nothing wrong with things as they are. From my perspective it seems that more and more rules/laws are applied to cater for the lowest common denominator. It may well be that all the legislation that has been brought in to counter the problems of child abuse, poor teaching, poor pupil attendance, health and safety and so on are necessary. But the fact remains that each new piece of legislation introduces extra work for Heads, management teams and staff and that takes them away from the classroom, or at least adds extra pressures on their time and energy. Time that could be better spent in the classroom, on the games field, in the art room or wherever else so many teachers give themselves unstintingly.

I do have concerns about the way education is heading, indeed about the way society is heading, because after all, the one is reflected by the other. Let me give one or two examples. Because of fears about child abuse it is now unacceptable to comfort a child by putting an arm round him or her. That such instinctive behaviour is forbidden seems to me outrageous nonsense. Sometimes it is necessary for a teacher to speak to a child privately so the child can talk in confidence. This too is difficult. Either there must be a second person available to see that nothing untoward happens, or the door must remain open so that all and sundry can see what is going on. In both instances it may be more difficult to discuss with the child something of a confidential matter.

As I stated earlier it was my belief that children of the age for whom I was responsible as a Housemaster (eleven to thirteen), should be allowed to go out without adult supervision as long as they were accompanied by at least one other person and had signed out in the book provided to indicate where they were heading. I have serious doubts whether I would allow this today if I was a Housemaster. In today's climate if anything goes wrong litigation is almost sure to follow. Moreover if the media get hold of the story it is necessary to find someone to blame. It appears 'accidents' don't happen these days. A scapegoat must always be found. Such stories of course, sell newspapers, which is one reason they are pursued. The litigation course is, I believe, too often followed because people see it as a means to a handsome payout. Of course this sort of occurrence is very sad. If money can alleviate the pain of someone who is injured or in some way make their lives easier well and good. But large sums of money are never going to bring anyone back. On the other hand there have been occasions when there has been gross negligence and those guilty have rightly been punished. But I still remain of the opinion that children need to let off steam. They need to be exposed to challenges which stretch them and by their very nature contain an element of danger.

A recent tragic case springs to mind. A child on a school outing died in a boat trip in Portsmouth Harbour. 'As the child's distraught mother said after the court hearing: "Too many mistakes were made bad decisions were taken and many safety measures were not adhered to."

All this is undoubtedly true and the school had little option but to plead guilty to breaches of health and safety regulations. A series of mishaps turned an exciting but hardly dangerous expedition into a disaster. The weather on that September day in 1999 was too rough for sailing so the master in charge took the nine children out in the school's dory. Its outboard failed, a boy fell over-board, and had to be hauled back in; as the boat was being paddled back to shore, taking water, a bucket containing a jellyfish tipped over. In the resulting pandemonium, the boat capsized.

Even this would not necessarily have been life-threatening, had the master had the presence of mind to count the heads. Alas, by the time they realized someone was trapped under the boat, it was too late. The anguish of both the teacher and the dead girl's parents can hardly be imagined.

The £2,000 fine imposed on the teacher surely reflected the judge's realization of the punishment he was inflicting on himself, since the tragedy marked the end of a 40-year teaching career. He had only gone out in the dory to assuage the disappointment of his pupils at having the sailing cancelled and until his dying day he will ask himself why he didn't count the heads as soon as he could.

With the benefit of hindsight, and the leisurely timetable of the law, it's easy to find fault. Why, the court was asked, did the school not conduct a risk assessment? Why was there no specific policy for sailing activities? Why had it not kept adequate maintenance records? Why had the teacher exceeded the Royal Yachting Association guidelines for the number of pupils under the supervision of one person?

The answer to all of the above questions is the same: because if all such questions about every activity were dealt with in such stupefying detail, the few teachers who were not driven mad by paperwork would have no time left to teach, let alone engage in anything more interesting.

Tighter health and safety rules have a cost, in addition to the obvious ones of massively increased bureaucracy. They stifle initiative, can produce additional risks of their own and, above all, alter the fundamental question, "Is this safe?", to "Does this comply with the rules?"' **

I can only add that there but for the grace of God go I. I imagine there are many of my generation out there who might say the same. I remember one Sunday taking a group of boys over the Clifton Suspension Bridge. We clambered over the parapet on the far side and slid down the steep muddy slope to the river. We then walked along the towpath till we came to one of the great slabs of rock on which protesters occasionally daub paint. It was quite steep and took us to the top of the gorge again. It was the sort of scramble that a family with active children wouldn't think twice about. But for one or two of the less athletic children it was a real challenge. The delight on their faces when they reached the top was reward enough. But if anything had gone wrong undoubtedly questions would have been asked.

Tightened rules and regulations and fear of litigation have made schools increasingly nervous about sending children on expeditions and outings. Fewer and fewer teachers will want to take the risk of being involved for fear of the consequences should something go wrong. Thankfully, at present, there are still those who are prepared to organize and supervise ski expeditions, water sports holidays, caving, rock-climbing and other activities. But their organization involves huge amounts of paper work which add considerably to the teachers' workload. Such outings provide

144

enjoyment, broaden the children's horizons, and often contain that element of danger which is so necessary. I believe passionately that should such outings and expeditions be withdrawn the children will be much the poorer for it. I have no doubt too that children less exposed to challenges will therefore be less able to cope with challenges and problems when they grow older.

Recently there has been a certain amount of press coverage following the death of a boy playing rugby. A school in Cambridgeshire has decided that rugby should no longer be played. Again the death of a child is tragic. But I do believe that banning boys from playing rugby is a retrograde step. Surely it is better that they express their aggression in the relative controlled arena of the rugby field than in the city centre on a Saturday night where they are even more likely to end up in hospital or worse?

My deafness has been a problem and if there is one thing that I would have changed in my life it is that I would have had perfect hearing. But who knows – I would have been a different person. Maybe I would not have followed a career in teaching. I do have concerns about the way education is going. Are we being too protective of our children? Can we reduce the amount of bureaucracy that envelops our education system? Can discipline be improved without the introduction of more rules and regulations? Do children have enough freedom and can we give back some of the freedom they used to have without endangering them?

Is teaching enjoyable any more? I count myself lucky that I began my career during a time when it was. But I suspect that many of those who are starting today will say it is still so. I hope this is the case. I have had a lot of fun over the years. Life for me has been like a kaleidoscope – full of many happy memories with only a very few best forgotten.

** From an article by Neil Collins in the Daily Telegraph on 4.11.2002